Using Instructional Objectives in Teaching

D. Cecil Clark
College of Education
University of Washington

Scott, Foresman and Company
Glenview, Illinois   *London*

Using Instructional Objectives in Teaching

To Robert Mager, for many hours long ago
and to Asahel Woodruff, for too many things.

Library of Congress Catalog Card Number: 72-79462
ISBN: 0-673-07620-2

Preface

Using Instructional Objectives in Teaching does not assume that a teacher who can write an instructional objective will automatically use it in teaching. It is, therefore, not simply a manual showing how to write instructional objectives; it is a book intended to help teachers more effectively use instructional objectives in their teaching. The author has repeatedly walked into school districts in which teachers, armed with manuals on "how to write instructional objectives," busy themselves by constructing long lists of specific and observable student outcomes. But, several months later, these same objectives have been filed away and quietly forgotten. That teachers do not use instructional objectives even after they write them is further manifested by the following types of comments: "I have learned to write an instructional objective; what do I do next?" or, "Are instructional objectives supposed to help me in my teaching? If so, how?" The existence of comments such as these, along with other observations, has led to the conclusion that developing skill in writing an instructional objective is one thing and using an instructional objective in actual teaching is quite another.

After some two years of rather frustrating attempts, the author has yet to discover any specific procedures teachers might follow in actually implementing instructional objectives in teaching. However, during that time, it has become rather clear that certain areas of concern must be given attention by teachers who plan to use instructional objectives. Likewise, some general and specific suggestions have been formulated that may provide starting points for teachers attempting to implement their objectives. It is around these areas that this book is organized. Both the areas of concern and the suggestions within each area have grown out of a large number of workshops on instructional objectives conducted by the author; in addition, they have come from teaching measurement and evaluation classes for prospective teachers, from difficulties encountered while working directly with teachers and curriculum designers as they have formulated and tried to implement instructional objectives, from vigorous and often unresolved discussions with colleagues, and from desperate invention when confronted by teachers working under production deadlines. The suggestions within each area of concern should not be mistaken for controlled research or as a distillation of the writings cited in the bibliography section. When more research is available, these suggestions will no doubt undergo modification and, in some cases, abandonment. In the meantime, teachers are encouraged to use them as working suggestions.

Though this book is written primarily for prospective and practicing teachers, it is also for curriculum designers and administrators, since in covering a variety of concerns, all related to the implementation of instructional objectives, it is inherently tied to curriculum organization as a whole. While every attempt has been made to keep discussion of the concerns straightforward and clear, some may appear complex and in need of thoughtful study. In view of this and also because some teachers may want a quick familiarization with instructional objectives preparatory to entering a "production" workshop, a condensed version of the book appears in Appendix A. It can be read easily in one sitting. Thus, the book can be read at two different levels: For a thorough and detailed understanding, the text itself should be studied; to pick up quickly and easily the essentials and specific suggestions for using instructional objectives, Appendix A and its referrals should be read. Whenever possible, you are encouraged to go through the book carefully and in depth; the more detailed discussions in the text proper, along with examples throughout the text and in the appendices, should provide a serious and exhaustive background.

Even though there has been an attempt to order the areas of concern logically, some can be studied quite independently of the rest. Therefore, you may choose to skip about through the various areas of concern; for continuity, however, you may want to follow the order presented. An extensive bibliography of the entire field of behavioral objectives has been included for additional and related reading. Since most of the material in this book has not been directly derived from these sources, few citations appear throughout the text.

As you work through the various areas of concern and suggestions within each, you will rather easily acquire skill in *writing* an instructional objective. More importantly, however, you will gain insight and suggestions as to how instructional objectives can actually be *used* in teaching. Based upon these areas of concern and suggestions, you are encouraged to go ahead and develop your own process for implementing instructional objectives in your teaching. This book should provide you with (1) greater confidence in the potential impact of instructional objectives on teaching, (2) knowledge of specific areas with which you must concern yourself as you actually begin to use instructional objectives, and (3) some suggestions for implementing instructional objectives in your teaching.

The author expresses appreciation to Dr. Percy Peckham for his thorough reading of Area of Concern 16, to Mrs. Jeanne Shelton for her expert help in typing the manuscript, and to the many students and teachers who constantly remind us of the reality and seriousness of public education. Finally, my wife and children have been patient, independent, and supportive during those hours alone.

D. Cecil Clark

Contents

Introduction

If education in general can be defined as bringing about intentional changes in the learner, then, more specifically, teaching should be the process of promoting or at least facilitating these changes. If such is the case, then teaching should be done carefully and well. While for many years teachers have been committed to change as the aim of teaching, they have done a less adequate job in identifying the changes they intend to produce and in examining the effectiveness of their teaching that is designed to bring about these changes. In other words, they have made accountability for changes in the student difficult.

The discussions that follow are ultimately aimed at helping teachers improve whatever it is they are doing to bring about change in their students; more accurately, to increase the precision of teaching. Why is this important? If teachers are finally to become professionals in the facilitating of change in students, then, like other professionals, they ought to be able to in fact bring about these changes and demonstrate that they have done so. Increasing the precision of their teaching will more readily enable them to do these two things. They are paid more and more as professionals, they are expected more and more to be professionals, and their ability to be more effective in facilitating change in students is needed more and more in this day and age.

The behavioral objectives "movement" is important because it will, as it matures, help increase precision in teaching. Minimally, it should help teachers more clearly designate changes that are socially desirable and that will help them determine the degree to which their teaching is facilitating these changes. Maximally, it should suggest specific steps in altering their teaching to more effectively bring about the changes. Such a strategy is an increase in precision.

What trends will grow out of this movement which will further help teachers increase the precision of their teaching? These are yet unclear. Importantly, however, the behavioral objectives movement should not be an end in and of itself, but rather a means to the end of greater precision in teaching. Let us view this as but one of many eventual phases educators will move through in becoming more precise in the professional business of teaching.

1

The behavioral objectives movement, with its initial formalization in the early writings of Ralph Tyler (e.g., 1931, 1934, 1950) was greatly accelerated with the Bloom-Group Taxonomies (1956, 1964) and made reachable to teachers through the colorful book by Robert Mager (1962). Over the past five or six years, more and more educators have moved from speaking about objectives to writing them. At the close of the 1960s, many attempts had been made to actually implement them. Now, a hard and exhaustive look at the whole business of behavioral objectives is probably more in order than finding some new educational fad with which to become enamored.

This book identifies "areas of concern" that have emerged among people working with objectives. Some of these areas have already received considerable thought and attention by people in the field; they are included because of their importance and because a more integrated approach may prove helpful to teachers. Other areas to be discussed have received little attention and have been too long neglected.

Area of Concern One:
How Shall We Define an *Objective?*

Surprising it is that during all the discussion over the past several years, few people have made any serious attempts to define precisely what they mean by "objectives," "behavioral objectives," "instructional objectives," and a host of other terms which they familiarly use. If we are to use objectives effectively, then, it would seem a most important area of concern to clearly define what we mean by an "objective."

When asked to define an "objective," many teachers easily respond with, "A behavioral objective is an observable activity of the learner." But this definition deals with a particular type of objective rather than objectives per se. Such an orientation is too narrow; we shall consider the characteristics of *any* objective, regardless of its type or form.

The definition that follows has proven to be understandable and workable for many teachers and should be sufficient until a better one comes along. Let us define an *objective* as an activity that includes the following characteristics:

1. The activity is engaged in by the learner, not by the teacher.
2. The activity identifies the learner's behavior.
3. The activity identifies the topic at which the behavior is directed.
4. The activity represents the consequences of some learning experience, not the learning experience itself.

1. The activity is engaged in by the learner, not by the teacher. This statement means that technically the teacher does not have an objective, or at least it is the same as the student's objective. Thus "The teacher will present the poem to the class" is not an objective because in this case the activity will be engaged in by the teacher rather than the learner. What is it then? It is simply a teacher activity, falling more legitimately into the category of instruction. This teacher activity can be turned into an objective as follows: "The student will be able to recite the poem (after it has been presented by the teacher)." Other examples of teacher activities which do *not* qualify as objectives are:

To develop an understanding of minority groups. (The implication is
   that the teacher is going to do something, not the student.)
To present a wider variety of experimental procedures to the class.
   (The teacher is doing the "presenting.")
To expose the students to contemporary painters. (The teacher is
.   doing the "exposing," but what is the student doing?)

2. The activity identifies the learner's behavior. Every objective
should identify the learner's behavior (again, not the teacher's). Suppose
we define *behavior* as *any* activity that can be engaged in by the learner.
This definition is most inclusive; it even includes behaviors that cannot be
seen.

At this point, it might be helpful to identify behaviors as being either
overt or covert in nature. *Overt* behavior is any behavior that can be
directly seen or heard by the teacher. *Verbally listing, writing on the
board, running, typing,* and *singing* are examples of overt behavior.
Covert behavior is any behavior that cannot be directly seen or heard by
the teacher. Examples are *thinking, problem solving, memorizing, appreciating,* and *valuing.*

Every objective must include the learner's behavior whether it is
covert or overt in form. An objective which identifies a covert behavior is
still an objective since the criteria of an objective depend on the presence
or absence of a behavior and not its form. "The student will be able to
recite a poem" and "The student will *know* a poem" are both legitimate
objectives.

When considering the above distinctions, caution should be taken
against thinking that a given behavior is always either covert or overt.
When placed in one objective, a behavior might be overt, but when
placed in another, covert. For example, "The student will *verbally list* the
last three presidents of the United States" is overt, while "The student will
mentally list the last three presidents of the United States" is covert. To
be sure, some behaviors are more often overt (e.g., listing) and some are
more often covert (e.g., valuing) in their use. To be on the safe side,
however, judgments about whether a given behavior is covert or overt
should be made only as it appears within a given objective.

3. The activity identifies the topic at which the behavior is directed.
Every objective should contain a topic. This can be either a *subject-
matter* topic (e.g., poem, whole numbers, robins, prejudice, gas expands
when heated) or a *skill* topic (e.g., buttonhole, volley, block, spin, weld).
Skills are more difficult to identify as topics because they are behaviors
themselves. That is, *buttonhole* can be thought of as both a behavior and
as a topic depending upon how it is used. If "buttonhole" is considered as
a unit in a sewing class (e.g., the buttonhole), then it is a topic; if
considered as an activity engaged in by the learner, as in "The student
can buttonhole a blouse," then "buttonhole" is the behavior, and
"blouse" is the topic.

At least one strategy can be used to minimize confusion caused by skill topics. Placing "the" in front of a skill makes it look more like a topic to be covered in class. Thus, the buttonhole, the volley, the block, the spin, the weld, can each be readily considered as the topic part of an objective. Following are examples of objectives with either subject-matter or skill topics (can you circle the behaviors directed at each of the topics?):

The student will be able to recite a *poem.* (subject-matter topic)
The student will be able to add *any two whole numbers.* (subject-matter topic)
The student will be able to identify *short stories.* (subject-matter topic)
The student will be able to describe *how gas expands when heated.* (subject-matter topic)
The student will be able to correctly complete *the buttonhole.* (skill topic)
The student will be able to correctly execute *the volley.* (skill topic)
The student will be able to demonstrate *the block.* (skill topic)
The student will be able to execute *the spin.* (skill topic)

4. *The activity represents the consequences of some learning experience, not the learning experience itself.* This characteristic ensures that the result of the instruction rather than the instruction itself will be the end product. Perhaps more than any of the above, this quality has posed the greatest problems in formulating objectives. Teachers, because they have for so long concentrated on the act of teaching itself, naturally tend to assume that "teaching" is the objective; but teaching is the means (the teacher activity), not the objective. An objective contains no instruction; it contains only the end product of that instruction. Some examples of instances in which the instructional experience has been mistaken for the consequences of the experience follow. These are instructional experiences, not outcomes, and do not qualify as objectives.

The student will go to the dairy.
The student will be exposed to the works of Mark Twain.
The student will hear the works of Bach.
The student will participate in field day.

What do these four examples have in common? They are all descriptions of some instructional activity or experience, but they only imply a hidden outcome (objective). If we ask teachers why they plan to take their classes to the dairy they might reply, "So the children will learn where milk comes from." The student's objective, then, is to understand where milk comes from rather than to go to the dairy. Each of the other examples can be easily converted into objectives by teasing out their hidden outcomes and stating these rather than the experience itself:

The student will be aware of the works of Mark Twain (after having been exposed to them).

The student will have an appreciation for the works of Bach (after having heard them).

The student will enjoy field days (after having participated in several of them).

Why is it important to have outcomes? After all, many would argue that the experience or the "process" is far more important than the product or outcome. That the experience itself may be far more crucial than the outcome is not the point in question, however. The point is that without an end there is no way to evaluate the appropriateness of an experience, that is, its effect.

Many teachers are more interested in "process" than they are in "product." This means they are more interested in the processes a student goes through while working toward a goal than they are in whether or not he achieves the goal. So be it; we can still have objectives. A process can be formulated into an objective (outcome) almost as easily as can a product; for example, "The student *will become more sensitive to the needs of others* as a result of having helped the group build a bridge." We would normally think of the italicized phrase as a process and the building of a bridge as a product. Building a bridge, teachers argue, is really not important; becoming more sensitive to the needs of others is what is important for the student. Yet in the example above, the process has been formulated as the objective. If we simply want a product objective, we might say, "The student will be able to build a bridge." Following are two more examples of process objectives: "The student *will have developed the ability to analyze a problem* as a result of being able to solve certain types of story problems," and "The student *will be able to identify his own strengths and weaknesses* as a result of having participated in three days of sensitivity training."

From the above discussion, we can see that there are hidden objectives that can be teased out of virtually any instructional experience and, more often than not, they will be acceptable to the very teacher who suggested the instruction in the first place.

By way of summary, an objective follows that illustrates the four characteristics that have been identified as found in objectives.

The student will be able to recite the poem "Down at the Sea."

(learner) (consequence) (behavior)   (topic)

(If you judge the above objective to be hopelessly trivial, consider this as a covert sign you are thinking ahead!)

**Suggestions for the Teacher Emerging
from This Area of Concern**

1. Before doing anything else, sit down and decide in advance what you will call an "objective." The definition should be clear and workable and apply to any objective, not just the more limited definition usually given to behavioral objectives.
2. Make certain you indeed have an objective—according to the definition—before starting to modify or improve it.

Area of Concern Two:
How Do Objectives Differ from Each Other?

First off, let us limit our discussion to those objectives which are most typically found in education and not be here concerned with such areas as business, law, medicine, or the like. What are the differences among various objectives in education? We can use a variety of dimensions in looking for these differences. For example, objectives differ in their participants: In some, the student is the learner; in others, the teacher is the learner (e.g., inservice workshops); in others, the administrator; and in still others, members of an entire school building or program may be involved. Objectives also differ in their importance and appropriateness, as well as in the time, money, and expertise required to teach them; they differ in topics, and so on.

For our discussion we shall consider primarily one dimension along which objectives differ—their form. The form of an objective can differ in two basic ways. First, an objective can be general and rather encompassing in scope, or it can be very specific and limited in scope. That is, objectives differ in their degree of generality and specificity. Second, an objective can be mostly overt and observable, or it can be mostly covert and unobservable. That is, objectives differ in their degree of overtness and covertness. It is important to note that these two differences in form can be relatively independent of each other. An objective can be very general or very specific and in either case be mostly overt or mostly covert. There is, however, a tendency for specific objectives to be more overt and for general objectives to be more covert. We shall examine these two differences in greater detail.

What is there about an objective that makes it general or specific in nature? The content and/or the behavior determine the degree of generality or specificity of the objective. For example, consider "The student will have developed an appreciation for literature." In this objective both the behavior and the topic are very general and inclusive. That is, *appreciation* no doubt includes a variety of different student behaviors (e.g., reading on his own, verbally expressing his liking of literature, acting enthusiastic about literature read, preferring literature over other types of reading), and *literature* includes many different topics (e.g., short stories, poetry, essays, novels). But consider the example

"The student will be able to define a compound sentence." In this objective both the behavior and the topic are limited and specific. Occasionally, a specific behavior will be combined with an inclusive topic (e.g., "The student will be able to list reasons for liking literature"), or an inclusive behavior will be combined with a specific topic (e.g., "The student will appreciate the comma"). But usually when one is general or specific, the other tends also to be general or specific.

Turning now to the second difference, as we discussed in Area of Concern 1, it is the *behavior*—viewed in the context of the objective—which determines the degree of overtness of an objective. In the example above, the behavior "appreciating" is mostly covert. By altering the objective slightly, however, we can make it more overt: "The student will verbally express an appreciation for literature."

Following are several examples which illustrate the general-specific and the covert-overt differences in form:

The student will be aware of the past presidents throughout history. (covert and general)

The student will verbally list the past three presidents of the United States. (overt and specific)

The student will be aware of the past three presidents of the United States. (covert and specific)

The student will be able to verbally list the past presidents throughout history. (overt and general)

It is the dimension of form which enables us to differentiate objectives by means of a rather simple classification scheme. If an objective is either (1) rather general and inclusive in scope, or (2) mostly covert, or (3) both, let us call it an *educational* objective, some examples of which follow.

1. The student will know some of the great poets in American history.
2. The student will be able to use math concepts in his daily living.
3. The student will demonstrate basic reading skills.
4. The student will exhibit more sensitivity to others.

Objectives such as those above are readily familiar to most teachers. Suppose, on the other hand, we have an objective which is (1) specific enough and (2) overt enough so we can clearly teach for it and determine when it has been attained; suppose also that (3) at least two more specific objectives can still be generated from it. Let us call an objective in a form meeting these qualifications an *instructional* objective. Following are some examples of instructional objectives (by comparing these with the four educational objectives above, you can see the increased overtness and specificity of instructional objectives):

1. The student will be able to identify several American poets living in the twentieth century and describe how their writings have influenced the American scene.
2. The student will be able to correctly pronounce most of the words when reading aloud any story assigned by the teacher.
3. The student will await his turn whenever the group is participating in any activity on the playground.
4. The student will be able to make the correct change for any transaction under ten dollars.

Note that the third characteristic of instructional objectives is present in each of the above: Each is left general enough so at least two more specific objectives can be generated. For example, consider instructional objective 4. From it we can still generate the following: "Given a customer buying an item which costs $2.39, the student will be able to make the correct change when given a $5.00 bill," or "Given an item costing $3.63, the student will be able to count out the correct change from a $5.00 bill."

Let us take a closer look at these last two objectives. Neither has any generating power left; that is, neither one allows us to generate two more specific objectives. Both are too specific and detailed. Whenever an instructional objective becomes so specific in form that we cannot generate at least two more specific objectives from it, it is no longer an instructional objective but rather a *drill* objective. This type of objective is exactly what its name implies, a simple rote objective. There is essentially a one-to-one correspondence between this objective and its instruction and evaluation. All three of these activities are virtually identical. For example, the instruction for the first drill objective above would be to repeatedly present the student with an item costing $2.39 and a $5.00 bill and tell him that the correct change would be $2.61. The evaluation would be about the same: The instructor would present an item costing $2.39 and a $5.00 bill paid by the customer, and ask the student what would be the correct change to give the customer. We are able to observe that the student obtains this objective through simple memory; he need not transfer, apply, or generalize his information.

Following are some additional examples of drill objectives, all of which are very specific and overt (compare these with instructional objectives 1, 2, and 3 above):

1. The student will be able to correctly state, on paper, that Robert Frost was the writer of "Death of the Hired Man."
2. The student will be able to correctly pronounce the following words: *pail, stoop, rolled, pulley,* and *atop.*
3. The student will refrain from shoving anyone in front of him when waiting in line to come in from recess.

By way of summary, three different categories of objectives have been described: *Educational, Instructional,* and *Drill.* The major difference among them is simply a matter of form; that is, a matter of the degree of their specificity and overtness. If an objective is rather encompassing or mostly covert or both, it is classified as an educational objective; if it is reasonably limited in scope and measurably overt, it qualifies as an instructional objective; if it becomes so limited in scope that additional objectives cannot be generated from it, it is called a drill objective.

The scheme of classifying objectives by form has been established simply to help the teacher make decisions about the most efficient level of specificity and overtness *for teaching purposes.* As is readily observable, educational objectives are too inclusive to provide specific guidelines for teaching or evaluation. Such objectives include so many potential outcomes that two teachers having the same educational objective may use entirely different teaching materials and procedures. To add to the problem, we have difficulty measuring when an educational objective has been attained. At the other extreme, drill objectives leave no room for alternatives or diversity in teaching and evaluation. They are rote and overly prescriptive. It seems, then, that instructional objectives, lying between the two extremes and giving guidelines with some flexibility, are the most practical for teaching purposes. Thus a teacher might say, "This objective is too much like an educational objective; perhaps we had better generate one that is a little more limited and somewhat more overt"; or "I think this objective is limited enough and overt enough to qualify as an instructional objective. Let's leave it the way it is"; or "We've gone too far by overworking this objective to the point that it is now a drill objective. Let's start working backwards to a slightly more inclusive objective." Indeed, one problem observed in working with teachers formulating objectives is that they spend too much time turning educational objectives into drill objectives rather than into instructional objectives.

Suggestions for the Teacher Emerging
from This Area of Concern:

Use the form of an objective as a guide; if its form is educational or drill and you want an instructional objective, more work is required.

Area of Concern Three:
How Are Objectives Related to Each Other?

In the last section we discussed the differences among objectives in education. A more difficult task is to describe relationships that exist among objectives and how these relationships can be used by the teacher. As there are various ways of looking at the differences among objectives, there are also numerous ways of looking at their relationships. We shall examine only those relationships that occur as the teacher goes about the task of developing objectives. These relationships exist (1) through the process of generation and (2) through the processes of sampling and inference. Both of these relationships will be described using Figure 1 on page 13.

Objectives Can Be Related to Each Other
Through the Process of Generation

Generally speaking, if from one or more objectives you create a new objective, you have engaged in the process of "generation." For example, suppose you have the objective, "The student will have developed an appreciation of literature." In asking yourself whether there are more specific objectives suggested by this one, you might generate the following: "On his own, the student will read at least two selections written by Mark Twain," and "When asked to write down his feelings about a selection read, the student will write more positive than neutral or negative impressions." For discussion purposes, it may be helpful to label the original objective a "parent" objective and the two generated ones "offspring"objectives. This will allow us to talk about one or the other without confusion.

The example just presented can be thought of as the generation of offspring from a parent, or a *downward* generation. Looking at Figure 1, if we started with educational objectives at the top and moved down through instructional objectives to drill objectives, we would be engaging in a downward generation, or a parent-to-offspring direction. However, it is possible to engage in the equally important activity of *upward* generation, or generation of a parent objective from several offspring objectives. For example, we might have offspring objectives *F, G,* and *H* before us

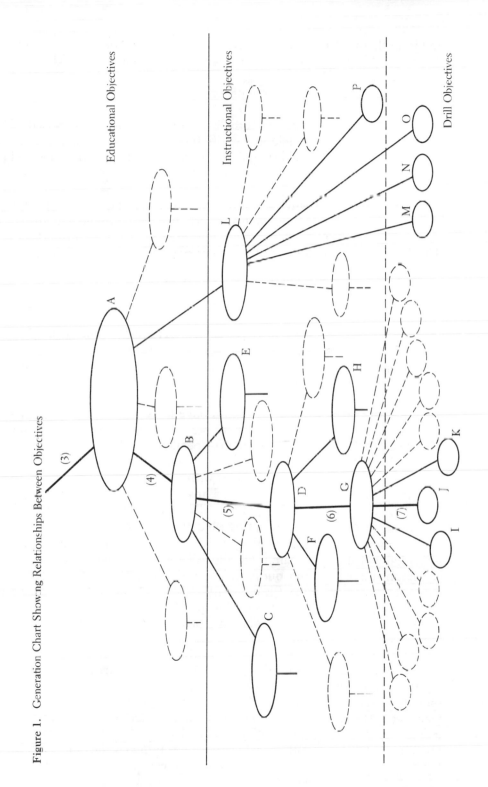

Figure 1. Generation Chart Showing Relationships Between Objectives

and from them ask if these three objectives suggest a more encompassing or general objective. As a result, we might generate objective *D*. This type of generation illustrates upward generation.

Suppose the following three offspring objectives:

The student will be able to verbally recite the poem "At the Seaside."
The student will be able to identify the meter used in the poem.
The student will be able to give an explanation for why the sea would come up no more.

After examining these three offspring objectives, we may decide that it is important to generate a more inclusive objective which would encompass these and several others which we might identify at some future time. Therefore, we might generate the parent objective:

The student will *know* the poem "At the Seaside."

What is the difference between a parent objective and an offspring objective? As we discussed in Area of Concern 2, the difference is simply a matter of degree. Offspring objectives tend to be more specific and limited and more overt than parent objectives. We can have parent and offspring objectives at both the educational and instructional levels. That is, parent objectives do not always have to be large educational objectives, and offspring objectives do not always have to be more specific instructional objectives. This is an important point to remember because many objectives that vary in their degree of specificity and overtness still fall under the general heading of instructional objectives; likewise with educational objectives. All objectives within these two levels can act as *both* parent and offspring objectives. Thus, objective *G* is an offspring of parent *D*, and *D* is an offspring of parent *B*, and so on. Going downward, *G* is a parent objective for offspring objectives *I, J,* and *K*.

Are there some objectives that will always be offspring objectives and some that will always be parent objectives? About the only thing that can be said in response to this question is that drill objectives will always be offspring objectives (since it is inherent in their definition that they have no generating power). Other than this qualification, we could enter any "generation" we wanted, designate one objective as a parent, and begin the process of generation.

The establishment of a "generation chart" is actually the process of at least one dimension of curriculum building. If a curriculum can be thought of, in part, as an ordered set of objectives (behaviors plus topics), then this generation and hook-up activity becomes most helpful to teachers. When completed, this network of objectives will provide a telling picture of this dimension of the curriculum. Holes can be spotted; branches overly laden with objectives can be trimmed while others can be filled out. It is important to keep in mind, however, that the completed pedigree chart will never appear neat and symmetrical; nor should it necessarily be that way. Some branches of objectives will be intentionally full and others rather light. It will, nonetheless, present teachers with an overall view of their just-completed work.

Objectives Can Be Related to Each Other Through the Process of Sampling and Inference

Sampling

Let us return to the parent objective, "The student will have developed an appreciation of literature," recalling the two offspring objectives that were generated. Could any additional offspring objectives be generated? Obviously, the answer is yes. Indeed, this particular parent objective is so general and inclusive that a great many offspring could be generated. These two offspring simply represent a sample of all those that *could have been* generated. The relationship here is between offspring that are generated and offspring that could have been generated.

Let us examine this concept of sampling more closely. Suppose we take one parent objective and present it to an infinite number of teachers, asking each to generate one "good" objective. We would end up with an infinite number of "good" offspring objectives from this one parent objective.

No doubt many of the teachers will have generated the same offspring objective. Thus, the population will include many repeats. Suppose we were to form a ranking of offspring. The most frequently occurring offspring would receive a rank of one, second most frequent a rank of two, and so on down the line. For our purposes here, suppose we concern ourselves only with the first few ranks; that is, we will be interested in only those offspring which were considered good by the greatest number of teachers. These we will call *prime* offspring.

The above theoretical discussion has important implications for the teacher. Suppose Mrs. Brown generates two offspring objectives from some designated parent objective. Is her sample *representative* of the hypothetical prime offspring for that particular objective? That is, are her two offspring similar to those that would be preferred by a large number of teachers? Obviously, this question can never really be answered. But Mrs. Brown would do well to ask herself this question anyway; it would cause her to think carefully about the appropriateness of the offspring objectives she generates. She would begin to place herself in the position of other teachers and even students by asking, "Would these be acceptable offspring objectives to other teachers in my area?" Teachers will find that the attempt to answer this question will bring about elimination and modification of many less suitable offspring objectives.

The concept of sampling can be reviewed through study of Figure 1. Look at instructional objective *G*, noting that offspring objectives *I*, *J*, and *K* have been generated from it. The dotted lines represent prime offspring that could be generated. The teacher needs to ask whether or not the sample *I, J,* and *K* would be considered representative of the twelve prime offspring that could be generated. That is, would *I, J,* and *K* be preferred or at least acceptable to a large number of teachers who teach for objective *G?*

Inference

The foregoing discussion on sampling leads us logically into a discussion about making inferences. Again, let us return to the parent objective, "The student will have developed an appreciation of literature." This is a rather broad educational objective. "Literature" is general and inclusive, and "appreciation" is covert and represents a great many different behaviors. Most educational objectives (like this one) suffer from being broad and unmeasurable (covert). This means that we, as teachers, end up inferring their attainment. The process goes roughly as follows: From the general and covert objective, we generate a sample of more specific and overt instructional objectives which we take as *evidence* for the attainment of the general objective. More precisely, if the student is able to attain the specific instructional objectives, we infer that he has also attained the general objective. Stated differently, there is no way to attain an educational objective (that is, no *measurable* way) except through the attainment of instructional objectives. In order to make inferences, we need something from which to infer—namely, overt instructional objectives. The process of generation allows us to establish a basis for making inferences. The relationship in this setting is between the observable objective (instructional) and the inferred objective (educational).

Whether teachers have instructional objectives or not, the process of "unconscious" inference goes on. Suppose our old educational objective about the student's development of an appreciation of literature. Teachers often draw conclusions about differences in appreciation among students. For example, how might a teacher conclude that Mary has developed a greater appreciation of literature than has Susan? Simply by the process of inference. But this process is often very haphazard and unconscious. Both Mary and Susan display before the teacher a large number of observable cues over a period of time. Typically, the teacher unconsciously selects a few, "adds" them up, and then makes an inference about Mary's and Susan's appreciation of literature. Examples of these cues might be widening of the eyes, quickness and pitch of the voice ("enthusiasm"), body posture when listening to a story ("attention"), number of books checked out from the library, activities engaged in during spare time, topics of conversation with classmates, comments by parents, and a host of others.

But the whole process is probably less systematic than this. Some of the cues used unconsciously would be rejected as evidence if brought into consciousness; sometimes the teacher manufactures cues when none are there; some inferences are based on very few cues while others require a large number.

Instructional objectives are really little more than the intentional formulation of cues that teachers have been using all along. In effect, they advertise the evidence (cues) upon which teachers make their inferences; and with instructional objectives, this evidence can be passed on to the students in advance! But, by doing this, will the students merely learn the cues and nothing else? By definition, teachers make a public commitment to accept these cues as evidence for the attainment of some nonmeasurable objectives; they must stick by this commitment once made. If they worry about their evidence as being too superficial, perhaps they should reexamine its appropriateness and depth. If a student demonstrates all the cues described, will teachers be willing to comfortably infer that the student has attained the greater part of the educational objective? They should.

Suggestions for the Teacher Emerging from This Area of Concern

The suggestions made here are for the generation of offspring objectives from a *single* parent objective; these are not to be confused with those presented in the next area of concern which deals with generating an entire curriculum of parent and offspring objectives.

1. Use any method for generating offspring objectives which is most workable for you; you should not become overly committed to or structured by any one approach. Place more emphasis upon examining offspring objectives once they have been generated and less emphasis upon the generation process itself.

2. Here are two methods for generating offspring objectives from a single parent objective. Many teachers have tried them with varying degrees of success.

Method 1: Breaking the parent objective down into more specific behaviors and topics. Suppose, again, our educational objective, "The student will have developed an appreciation of literature." Method 1 involves breaking down both the behavior and the topic. Thus, "appreciation" might include such behaviors as reading on his own, making positive verbal statements, conversing about topics read in class, describing the lives of various authors, and so on. "Literature" might include poetry, short story, novel, and so on.

After you have broken down the objectives into as much detail as possible, you should place the topics in some logical order. Next, you should match up the topics with some of the behaviors, thereby formulating objectives. The idea here is to generate as many objectives as possible from the pool of topics and behaviors.

In the next step, you should adjust and modify the objectives until they appear more appropriate and representative. In the process you will add some, eliminate some, and change some. (See Appendix C for examples.)

Method 2: Using the shotgun approach. This is a rather straightforward and simple approach that has turned out to be surprisingly helpful. You should place the parent objective before you and, with abandon, generate as many offspring as possible. At this initial stage you should not worry about how appropriate the offspring are, how measurable they are, or whether or not they are specific enough. Simply produce. After this stage, go back and delete, add, and modify the offspring which have been generated. You should replace those that are too general with more specific ones, make all measurable, and eliminate the unimportant ones. (See Appendix C for examples.)

3. Regardless of the generation method used, all your offspring objectives should be limited enough and overt enough so that (1) they guide the selection of instructional materials and suggest teaching activities, (2) they give the student reasonably clear direction for his study and effort, and (3) their attainment can be readily determined.

4. After the offspring objectives have been generated and refined, you should try them out on a sample of students and again modify them before they are implemented.

5. Generally, you can do a more thorough job by generating from a parent objective than by generating off the top of your head. This latter activity too frequently yields haphazard and piecemeal results.

6. You should not become discouraged when you are unable to generate satisfying offspring for *all* your parent objectives. As a result of being scolded for having nonmeasurable objectives, some teachers have moved to the other extreme, throwing the baby out with the bath. Unless a complete set of highly measurable offspring can be generated from a parent objective, some teachers have thrown out that parent objective regardless of its importance. If a parent objective is important but mostly nonmeasurable, you should use it anyway. At least one or two measurable offspring can be generated from *any* parent objective. For now, be willing to live with objectives that are only partially measurable.

7. If you want instructional objectives, you should try to stop ending up with drill objectives. Some teachers have gone from one extreme to the other; from general, fuzzy, and unattainable objectives to minute, overly detailed, and stifling objectives. Both extremes are unworkable in the classroom. Some teachers have become so compulsive about adhering to the mechanics of writing "behavioral" objectives that the means (writing objectives) have become the end. Furthermore, every instructional objective does *not* have to begin with "Given such and such . . . " or "Without the aid of . . . " These and other conditions that must exist when the learner demonstrates the behavior often tend to clog up the objective. Also, stating how well the behavior must be performed need

not be present in an instructional objective. This level of acceptable performance will vary considerably from group to group and even from student to student. As a rule of thumb, stop generating downward while offspring objectives can still be turned into parent objectives. This will prevent you from going too far and ending up with drill objectives.

8. You should probably spend most of your time generating off-spring from objectives that are within the instructional level. Parent objectives within the instructional level will turn out to prescribe more definite instruction than parent objectives within the educational level. Thus, in Figure 1, parent objective D would be more helpful than parent objective A.

9. You should continually check to make sure your offspring objectives are more specific and more overt than your parent objective. Thus, are F, G, and H more specific and overt in D?

10. If generation is occurring at several different levels (e.g., levels 4, 5, and 6 in Figure 1), try to ensure that the offspring at each level are all about the same degree of specificity. That is, C, D, and E should be about the same degree of specificity as should F, G, and H. This procedure facilitates relating objectives to each other.

11. You should try to generate offspring objectives a level at a time rather than skipping levels. For example, in Figure 1, offspring objectives C and E are close to parent objective B in their level of specificity; however, offspring objectives M, N, O, and P are rather far removed from parent objective L. That is, they are very specific and L is very general—the jump from M, N, O, and P to L has been a large one.

Why are small steps preferred over large leaps? If you start with a very general objective and generate very specific objectives, you will find, more often than not, that the generated objectives turn out to be unsatisfying and inexhaustive evidence for the attainment of the general objective. On the other hand, if you generate objectives in small steps, making them a little more specific each time, you will achieve more complete and more satisfying objectives. Consider the objective "The student will have developed an appreciation of literature." Suppose, from this parent, you generate this offspring: "The student will listen closely, and react orally, to his fellow students' opinions of various aspects of *Huckleberry Finn*." You have jumped from the very general to the very specific. Most teachers would consider this specific objective to be a rather incomplete and weak bit of evidence that the student really appreciates all of literature.

But suppose you have worked your way down level-by-level from the very general objective. Your objective at some in-between level might be "The student will have gained an appreciation of the writings of Mark Twain." With this more limited parent objective, your above offspring would make more sense. If you had additional offspring like "In essay form, the student will compare attributes of any of Twain's characters to those of his own personality," "On his own, the student will read another selection written by Mark Twain," and "After reading *Huckleberry Finn*, the student will describe the main events of the plot," plus a few more, your more limited parent objective would take on even more meaning. In sum, you should not jump from educational objectives immediately down to drill objectives. Such a procedure is of little help in preparing overall instruction.

12. In generating offspring objectives, try to be representative rather than exhaustive. Teachers unaware of the concepts of sampling and inference have spent countless hours attempting to generate all possible offspring from a given parent objective. This kind of exhaustiveness is unnecessary. If you can make a comfortable inference from the attainment of five carefully selected offspring objectives, why insist upon twenty? Additionally, you will never be able to generate all possible offspring. At present, then, the best strategy appears to be that of generating several representative offspring from a parent and then stopping.

13. You should realize that one set of offspring objectives is probably just as acceptable as some other set. Worrying about which set of offspring is most like the "true" set of offspring is unnecessary and unrealistic. This concern usually arises when a group of teachers gathers for the purpose of developing curriculum objectives. They all start working from the same parent objective. After a few minutes one teacher will read several offspring just generated. Another teacher in the group will express some uneasiness and say, "That's not *really* what appreciation is." Following this statement, lively discussion ensues about the true nature of "appreciation."

Such a discussion among teachers turns out to be a philosophical issue about reality. Do we take an absolute position or a relative position? If we take the former, we would ask, What are the real offspring objectives? If we take the latter, we would ask, What shall we have as offspring objectives?

For the purposes of this book, the most functional orientation will be to generate offspring objectives which are acceptable to a sample of teachers in one's own area, setting aside the question of "true" offspring. Also, teachers should be a little more willing to accept offspring which differ from their own.

14. An orientation in which you view *every* objective as being tied into a more general objective may prove helpful. One implication of this orientation is that almost all drill objectives can be tied to some instructional and/or educational objective. Suppose the drill objective, "The student will be able to correctly sharpen a pencil." Even though one might argue that this objective is useful in and of itself, it can be tied to a more general study-skill objective. Thus, you may want the student to be able to sharpen his pencil so he can practice writing so he can move through school and, as a result, obtain a job. Assuming such an orientation will help you continually connect drill objectives to instruc-

tional objectives and thence to educational objectives. This attempt to "tie together" objectives should help with the difficult problem of prerequisite skills.

15. In those cases where offspring objectives turn out to be rather far removed from the parent objective (refer back to suggestion 11), the representative sample should be larger than in those cases where offspring are close to the parents. Thus, if a long inference is going to be made, then the evidence (number of offspring objectives) should be more complete.

Area of Concern Four:
How Are Objectives Generated for an Entire Unit or Course?

This area of concern has received little if any attention by writers in the field. Writing down specific and measurable objectives simply to show mastery of a skill is one thing, but it is quite another to roll up your sleeves and attempt to use this skill in writing objectives for an actual unit or course. In this area there is a desperate need for knowledge about specific and workable models to follow in generating objectives for an entire unit or course. Unfortunately, as of now these models are virtually nonexistent.

The two methods described in this section are not to be mistaken for well-developed models; they have grown out of a series of workshops in which teachers have been faced with the awesome task of developing entire curricula based upon an objectives approach. They have proven rather helpful when used separately or in combination; their description will constitute suggestions emerging from this area of concern.

In the last section, methods 1 and 2 (pp. 17–18) for generating offspring objectives from a single parent objective were described. The purpose was to illustrate the basic strategy of generation. In this section we will want to apply that strategy in generating large numbers of instructional objectives from many parent objectives. The two methods to be described here are simply an expansion of method 1 of the previous section.

Topic Display Method

Recall the definition of a "topic" in Area of Concern 1. Briefly, it is anything that is taught by the teacher, usually in the form of subject-matter topics or skill topics. Topics are most often in the form of a concept, a main idea, a principle or generalization, or simply bits of information. That is, if we were to pick up a new "scope-and-sequence" chart, a curriculum guide, a textbook for the student, or a teacher edition of that text, we would observe the topics to be in these various forms. Differentiating concepts from principles or main ideas is not our task in this section; it is important, however, to differentiate all of these from objectives. Topics in whatever form they appear do not contain behaviors and are not, therefore, objectives. This is an important point. A concept or a main idea, if it does not mention the student's behavior—and it seldom does—is not an objective.

In using the topic display method, a first and very important step for you as a teacher is to gather and display all of the topics you plan to teach. There are a variety of sources that can be used for gathering these topics. You may simply sit down and from your experience list all of the topics you plan to teach; or you may cull these topics from your lesson plans and discussion outlines; or you may go to curriculum guides published by the district, to various textbooks and programs that are available for use, or to virtually any source you choose. The important point is that you bring together all possible topics you plan to teach in a given class. Teachers using this method have generally found that listing rather specific topics is preferred over listing more general topics. The reason for this is that if the topics are specific and detailed, teachers can more easily identify which topics have been omitted and which need to be placed together. The final display typically includes topics which vary somewhat in their degree of specificity. This is mostly unavoidable and should be of little concern as long as the topics as a group are reasonably specific.

Once these rather specific topics are decided upon, you should attempt to impose some order or sequence upon them. Since the sequencing of objectives is covered in Area of Concern 10, it will be mentioned only briefly here. The topics might be ordered in terms of what you feel to be a logical order, or in terms of their difficulty, or in terms of some other criteria. The important point is that, whenever possible, ordering does occur. (Many teachers have found a generation chart similar to Figure 1 on page 13 to be helpful. Rather than a network of objectives, they first develop a network of interrelated topics and then formulate each into an objective. This network usually extends over a complete year or several years.)

After ordering the topics, the next step is to combine them with behaviors, thereby formulating objectives. If the topics are reasonably specific before this phase begins, you will have a greater tendency to end up with objectives which qualify as instructional objectives and, as such, need no further refinement.

What behaviors are to be assigned to each topic? The author has struggled with this question for the past several years. Initially it was felt that for every topic several different "levels" of objectives should be manufactured. These levels were taken from the Bloom-Group Taxonomies. Thus, for any given topic, teachers were encouraged to generate a *knowledge* objective, a *comprehension* objective, an *application* objective, and so on. This suggestion all too frequently produced confusion and a generally unrealistic and make-work task. (See Area of Concern 15 for a more complete discussion of the Bloom-Group Taxonomies.)

The above procedure was simplified when teachers were encouraged to generate only two or three "levels" of objectives for each topic rather than the six prescribed by the taxonomies. This still turned out to be a difficult and unhelpful activity. Finally, teachers were simply told to employ whatever behaviors *they* felt were important and not to worry so much about existing taxonomies of behaviors. This suggestion had not been offered earlier because of a concern that teachers might generate only "low-level" rote (drill) objectives, and omit a great many other "higher-level" (instructional) ones. This concern turned out to be unwarranted, especially when teachers were encouraged to think about *all* types of objectives they considered important which could be generated for a particular topic.

At this point in time, the most plausible strategy seems to be for teachers to generate any objectives they consider important and useful for given topics.

The display of topics is expanded, consolidated, and rearranged during the process of generating the complete objectives. Sometimes several objectives will be generated for one topic; other times, when the topics are broken down into considerable detail, several will be consolidated into one objective. However you move through this phase, it is important that when you finish, you have a rather satisfying set of objectives. Here again, as was mentioned earlier, you need to think in terms of generating a representative set of objectives rather than an exhaustive set.

Perhaps the main difficulty teachers encounter when using this method is in deciding what form the topics should take. A biology teacher will frequently list topics in the form of concepts or principles and generalizations; a history teacher often lists topics in the form of bits and pieces of information. Teachers ask, Should my topics be in the form of concepts, in the form of principles or generalizations, in the form of simply factual material, or what? Should I be consistent all the way through my topics? Up to this point, the author has been unable to muster much evidence that the form makes any difference at all or that a teacher needs to be consistent all the way through topics. Some teachers feel more comfortable listing their topics in the form of concepts and generalizations, while others prefer listing them simply as bits and pieces of information. Likewise, some teachers want to be consistent in form and others give little thought to it. What does seem to be important is that the topics are completely covered in the objectives, that the objectives are generally representative of those that could be generated, and that you, the teacher, are satisfied with them.

If the topics are sequenced, then the resulting list of objectives will likewise be sequenced and in order for instructional purposes. (See Appendix C for examples of this method.)

Downward Generation Method

This method simply expands the generating of several offspring objectives from a single parent objective (review Figure 1). Here you start with several broad, important educational objectives and carefully generate downward from each one. After generating down to an instructional level for one objective, you repeat the process with another and another. After this has been accomplished, you can go back and reassign some of the offspring to different parents, and generate additional offspring and parents. An attempt should be made to be more exhaustive in generating at a very general level and more representative in generating at more specific levels. With the exception of this slight modification, suggestions made in Area of Concern 3 are applicable here. (See Appendix C for examples of this method.)

What are the differences between these two methods and which is to be preferred? With the topic display method, rather specific objectives are generated from a set of topics; with the downward generation method, specific objectives are generated from general objectives. Often teachers planning specific units prefer the topic display method whereas district-wide curriculum planning committees often prefer the downward generation method. Other people prefer and use some combination of both. Perhaps the rule of thumb at this point should be to use whichever method or combination fits most easily in a particular situation and accomplishes the job.

Area of Concern Five:
Why Have Instructional Objectives?

Suppose one hundred teachers were randomly selected from the population of teachers in the United States and asked, Do you use objectives in your teaching? Certainly the overwhelming reply would be yes. If this is the case, why the increasing emphasis upon using *instructional* objectives? (If you do not recall the conditions that must be met for an objective to qualify as an instructional objective, see page 3.) Teachers have rightfully asked this question over and over again, and some of the replies are both amusing and startling. For example, "Well, instructional objectives are in vogue right now, and you should at least be able to talk about them!" or "You should have instructional objectives because having them is better than not having them," or "It should be obvious that having instructional objectives produces better results than not having them." All too often enthusiasts in this area are more concerned with crusading than they are with responding with carefully thought-through answers to legitimate questions. The majority of claims made by proponents are at once intuitively reasonable, uncomfortably overstated, and mostly without significant research support (see Area of Concern 16).

One would certainly be naive in believing that instructional objectives represent the only or perhaps even major solution to our difficulties in helping students to learn. Nor should one mistakenly view instructional objectives as having been systematically developed and carefully researched. In their present state of undevelopment, they do not represent a powerful new approach to teaching, and some of their limitations and disadvantages are serious ones. If instructional objectives are to ultimately make a significant contribution to education, it will only be after patient and rigorous development and evaluation by all concerned.

In the meantime, is there sufficient justification for the discriminate use of instructional objectives by teachers in certain areas and for certain purposes? Yes, there is. The justifications that follow are not meant to be exhaustive nor complete, but they are some of the more important ones. They are specific enough to be useful and particularly relevant to the more pressing interests and problems teachers experience in the classroom. They are tentative statements arising from anecdotal reports, survey results, discussions with teachers and students, writers in the field, and observations resulting from several years of teaching college classes by instructional objectives.

Justifications for the Use of Instructional Objectives

If instructional objectives are used, then the following should happen:

1. The teacher will have a method by which to measure, at least partially, important objectives not measured in the past.
2. The teacher and the student will have greater visible evidence that the objectives have been achieved.
3. The student will experience considerably more freedom in achieving an objective.
4. The student will feel greater focus and direction on what is important, on what to study for, and on what he will be evaluated.
5. In the long run, both the teacher and the student will save time and energy.
6. The student will participate more in his own instruction.
7. The teacher will feel greater security with this more direct evidence of "teaching effectiveness."

1. The teacher will have a method by which to measure, at least partially, important objectives not measured in the past. One of the more serious criticisms of instructional objectives has been that, by having them, teachers end up with only those that are easily measured. And, as it turns out, easy-to-measure objectives *are* frequently trivial and unimportant. Thus, teachers have omitted crucial and difficult-to-define objectives in favor of the unimportant. While this criticism is now becoming less widespread, it is still a valid one. It may, however, point out our inexperience in formulating instructional objectives more than an inherent weakness in their use.

To be sure, initial experience in developing instructional objectives has produced many objectives which are measurable but trivial. However, on the positive side, this same strategy can be used to make more measurable important objectives that have been left unmeasured in the past. Briefly, here is how it can work.

Suppose a teacher has the following simple instructional objective: "The student will, most of the time, refrain from making loud noises and disrupting those around him whenever in a line." This is an overt objective, easily measured, and perhaps not earthshaking in importance. Suppose also that this same teacher considers the following as far more crucial but mostly unmeasurable: "The student will become more sensitive to those around him." How could this educational objective be taught for and measured? (If you do not recall the distinction between educational and instructional objectives, see page 9.)

If teachers can generate a representative sample of instructional objectives that they are willing to accept as evidence for the educational objective, then they can now teach for and measure it; and, if the student achieves these, he will have, in effect, achieved the educational objective. Thus, refraining from making loud noises and disrupting those around him might be one of several instructional objectives which, when taken as a group, will represent a student's becoming more sensitive to those around him. If teachers are willing to permit the attainment of a carefully selected sample of instructional objectives to represent at least the partial attainment of an educational objective, they are in a position to start measuring some aspects of *all* objectives.

2. *The teacher and student will have greater visible evidence that the objectives have been achieved.* Suppose a teacher has the following objective: "The students will have developed an awareness of the various minority groups in the United States." With this in mind, he presents material on several different minority groups, raises questions for group discussion, encourages students to visit the homes of minority groups in the community, provides role-playing activities, and a variety of other "exposures." He then administers a test asking students factual material about minority groups in the United States.

When asked if his students have achieved the objective he will often reply, "I hope so," or "I would say so, yes," or "It's just too early to tell; this awareness cannot come about overnight." If the student is asked whether he has developed an awareness of various minority groups what can he say? "I guess so," or "Oh, I suppose so," or "How should I know?"

The all-too-frequent result of such an experience is that the teacher and the student are left with the hope or belief that some "awareness" has been developed. This teacher did not take the time and effort to decide upon what kinds of overt evidence he would accept for "awareness." It is this fuzzy and unsure feeling that instructional objectives are designed to reduce and often eliminate.

It is entirely possible for a teacher, using instructional objectives, to become more sure about what is being attained but, at the same time, experience greater frustration. Those less important objectives which a teacher can see actually being attained may not be satisfying evidence for the attainment of more important covert objectives. For example, a teacher has no trouble determining whether or not a student can "verbally describe the living patterns of various minority groups in the United States," but, alas, this may not be very satisfying evidence that the student has developed a genuine "awareness" of these minority groups.

The best solution to this dilemma is to generate more complete and satisfying evidence of "awareness." Until this can be done, however, teachers may take comfort in knowing for certain that their students have achieved at least some objectives. The frustration teachers feel in not being able to generate completely satisfying instructional objectives should be less than that experienced in having little or no visible evidence for their important educational objectives.

3. *The student will experience considerably more freedom in achieving an objective.* For a detailed discussion of the relationship between instructional objectives and individual differences, you are directed to Area of Concern 13. Some parts of that discussion are considered relevant to this justification and will be presented here.

There are at least two ways individualized instruction can occur with the use of instructional objectives. A teacher might sit down with each student and, based upon his abilities and background, construct a unique set of objectives tailored to that student's needs. This approach calls for some modification in the more traditional structure of one teacher providing instructional experiences for some thirty students. If each student works on his unique set of ten objectives, one teacher would be working with three hundred different objectives simultaneously. No single teacher could be asked to assume such a responsibility! This type of individualizing requires a group of teachers, a large variety of teaching materials, and an entirely new management system.

A second type of individualizing, more workable in the existing educational structure, is to provide the student with several alternative paths to reach the same objective. All students are required to attain the same set of "core" objectives, but each is free to use any approach which is most comfortable for him. For example, a student may choose to attend a formal class presentation, listen to tapes in his own home, view film presentations in the film laboratory, attend group discussion sessions, read outside materials, or whatever combination of these that suits him. With this approach, the teacher could go one step further and provide optional or "enrichment" objectives for those students who easily attain (or cannot attain) the "core" objectives.

How does either approach permit the student greater freedom? If the student, before beginning instruction, has clearly in mind what he is supposed to be able to do at the end of his instructional experiences, he is in a much better position to make decisions about how he can best go about attaining the objective. If he is an older student, he usually has a clearer view of his own repertoire and what past learning and experience can be brought to bear on the present objective than does the teacher. After examining his background as it relates to the objective, he can more effectively "pick and choose" from the instructional experiences available for that particular objective. Herein lies his greater freedom.

How does the typical classroom setting prevent this freedom? First, the student does not usually know in advance what his end behavior is supposed to be; second, the teacher usually teaches to the student with the "average" repertoire. Unfortunately, such an approach tends to prevent the student from *helping* the teacher; he can discover his end behavior only bit by bit and no faster than the day-to-day instruction. Thus, he is actually "contained" in the absence of this knowledge.

On the other hand, anecdotal evidence seems to suggest that with instructional objectives students begin to spread themselves out in terms of rate of achieving the objectives and type and variety of materials used. They do not seem to exhibit as much "spread" or variability in the degree of attainment of the objective. Thus, with objectives, the greatest variability seems to occur within the means and not the ends; in the more traditional approach the variability seems to occur more in the ends, not the means.

4. The student will feel a greater focus and direction on what is important, on what to study for, and on what he will be evaluated. Surveys and anecdotal reports taken by the author consistently suggest that specific direction and focus is the major advantage that comes from using instructional objectives. If students have a set of objectives, they appear to be less frightened and anxious when given a large list of references or resource materials because now they read and study selectively in working toward the objective. At the same time, the students are aware that in achieving the objectives they are also preparing rather specifically for their evaluation.

Suppose, for example, the following instructional objective: "The student will be able to add any two single-digit numbers." This objective provides clear direction and focus; the student is able to concentrate on learning to add any two single-digit number combinations from zero to nine. He does not worry about numbers greater than nine or any other operation than addition.

When asked what they felt was the major disadvantage in using instructional objectives, a small percentage of students reported they were too limiting. Some students felt it was a disadvantage to study for only the objective, passing over important but unrelated material; they were "trying to reach the objective" rather than "studying the material." This concern about an overfocus is a legitimate one and suggests at least two cautions when using instructional objectives. First, if a student is to limit his study only to the objectives stated, considerable care must be taken to make certain these objectives are in fact important. There are a large number of different objectives a student can work toward in a given course, but there is only so much time. Because of this limitation, teachers must discriminate in selecting objectives so that time is spent on worthwhile ones; usually, students cannot afford the luxury of meandering among less important objectives.

A second caution involves the nature of the objective. If teachers want students to "study more widely" and resist focusing on very specific topics and behaviors, they must revise the objectives themselves to ensure this branching-out activity; they would certainly not want a group of drill objectives in this case. Suppose a teacher had developed the following drill objective: "The student will be able to add two plus two." The focus here is excruciating! The student simply memorizes one association and nothing else: 2 + 2 = 4. Most teachers would clearly want the student to study more widely. Thus, the objective should be revised to an instructional one: "The student will be able to add any two single-digit numbers." Now the student would have to study not only 2 + 2 = 4, but also 3 + 1 = 4, 7 + 6 = 13, 9 + 2 = 11, and so on.

To be sure, even the above revised objective may appear painfully focused in actual practice. It was chosen because it was a clear and simple illustration. Slight revisions of almost any drill objective into an instructional one can immediately make it more inclusive so the student will have to study more widely. (A good rule of thumb is to stay away from drill objectives.) Revisions are simple and very effectively accomplished. As it turns out, this "limiting" nature of an instructional objective can be quickly reversed and need not represent a disadvantage. Indeed, suppose the following objective: "The student will be able to describe the plots and other details of not less than twenty-five short stories he can find in the library."

5. In the long run, both the teacher and the student will save time and energy. For the teacher, instructional objectives will save time and energy by providing greater direction in (1) selecting instructional materials, (2) planning learning activities, and (3) evaluating student learning. An example may serve to illustrate.

Suppose there are two different teachers going about their teaching activities. Mrs. Brown has as one overriding objective for her students: "The student will be aware of contemporary composers." Even though this objective is not written down in her lesson preparations, it is always in the back of her mind. Her first task is to select materials for the topic. Since her objective is rather inclusive and covert, she has no clear guidelines for accepting or rejecting any given materials as being relevant or irrelevant. As a result, considerable time and energy are expended in deciding what should be selected and what should be left out. For example, which composers are to be considered as contemporary? Should only those who are primarily composers be selected? Should all of the major types of contemporary music be included? And so it goes. After deciding upon the content materials to be presented, Mrs. Brown must now decide how they will be presented and in what sequence. Should the musical selections be covered first, followed by a discussion of various types of contemporary music, or vice versa? Should the composers and their life histories first be presented, followed by several examples of their music, or vice versa? And so on. Finally, Mrs. Brown must decide upon some type of evaluation of her students' "awareness of contemporary composers." Should they be given true-false items on the lives of the composers? Should they be asked to give their personal reactions to the various types of contemporary music? Should they be asked to identify various types of music and match each type with a composer? And so on.

The above procedures followed by Mrs. Brown are not unlike those followed by many teachers in planning instructional units. Importantly, each of the foregoing decisions must be made no matter what strategy is used by a teacher. However, the time and energy required in making these decisions will differ from strategy to strategy. Because her objective was rather inclusive and covert in nature, Mrs. Brown really had no clear guidelines to follow in making these decisions. As guidelines became less clear, more time and energy was required in decision making.

Suppose Mrs. Jones, a second teacher, has the following instructional objectives. "The student will be able to:

1. Describe the major events in the lives of the following composers (a group is suggested);
2. Describe the musical style of each of these composers;
3. Identify a given composer's style when listening to his compositions;
4. Identify the composer when listening to a *new* group of compositions from these composers;
5. And so on."

Mrs. Jones puts in considerably more time and energy identifying and clearly writing her instructional objectives than does Mrs. Brown with her unwritten educational objective.

Mrs. Jones' next step is to select instructional materials. Since her objectives are limited, clear, and communicable, the relevance of any given material can be easily and quickly determined. For example, material about contemporary composers other than those included in her group will be mostly omitted. Likewise, sources describing each of the selected men along with their compositions must be secured. Her next step is to decide how the materials are to be presented and in what sequence. Here again, the objectives save her time and energy. For example, objective 1 suggests that she might describe the major events in the lives of composers. Objective 3 suggests that she might play several compositions by a given composer, identifying his style in each. Since Mrs. Jones earlier took the time to place her instructional objectives in what she considers an appropriate sequence, she now simply parallels that sequence in her instruction. That is, moving from objective 1, to 2, and on through 5.

Mrs. Jones must now plan evaluation. Again, since her objectives are specific and overt, they readily prescribe evaluation. Her task is merely to develop an instrument that calls forth the same behaviors and topics that have been described in the objectives. To evaluate the students' attainment of objective 4, for example, she simply presents them with a new group of compositions from these composers and asks for an identification of the composer. Not only is the evaluation planning carried out quickly and easily, it also turns out to have reasonable validity.

In sum, Mrs. Brown and Mrs. Jones have made essentially the same decisions in selecting instructional materials, planning learning activities, and developing evaluation; but Mrs. Jones expends less overall time and energy because of the directing nature of her specific and overt instructional objectives.

Using instructional objectives will also save time and energy for the student by presenting him with a clear picture of the topics to be studied and the behaviors which he is to demonstrate relative to those topics. In the above instructional objectives developed by Mrs. Jones, his study will be concentrated on the following topics:

Major events in the lives of certain composers
Musical style of each of these people

He will be required to demonstrate only the following behaviors:

Describing
Identifying through listening

By way of contrast, what topics would he need to study and what behaviors would he need to display if he were to study the unit prepared by Mrs. Brown? Since he is exposed to her instruction only and not to any objectives (which, in this case, turn out to provide little direction anyway), the student has little direction in determining just what to study. Thus, instructional objectives tend to focus the student's efforts in specific areas and at the same time prepare him for his evaluation.

6. *The student will participate more in his own instruction.* Too often teachers unintentionally prevent the student from playing more than a minor role in his own instruction. To be sure, one can walk into almost any classroom today and observe the students actively engaged in some activity designed by the *teacher*. But this is quite different from asking the *student* to think up and engage in some activity which will help him achieve his objective. At its worst, the student participates in the teacher's instructional presentation and not his own instructional experience.

By having a clear understanding of objectives intended for him as opposed to a clear understanding of what the teacher *plans to cover*, the student can become more involved in helping the teacher change student behavior. This will be a more effective approach for at least two reasons. First, the student can selectively call upon his own background, with the objectives before him, and help make decisions about the appropriateness of various teacher-planned experiences. Second, his motivation in the learning experience is likely to increase. This will result from a feeling of greater responsibility for his own behavioral changes and also a feeling that the teacher respects him more, having given him greater charge over his own learning. Furthermore, some motivation will result from simply presenting the student with an "end point" toward which he can work. (Some would argue that instructional objectives might produce "task oriented" students.)

7. *The teacher will feel greater security with this more direct evidence of "teaching effectiveness."* Suppose "teaching effectiveness" is in part defined as the degree to which a teacher can bring about student attainment of the objectives. (These objectives might have been generated by the teacher, by the students, or a combination of both.) Regardless of the nature of the objectives, a teacher's effectiveness or success is represented by the degree to which his students attain the objectives.

At least two problems exist with current teacher-evaluation forms. First, the characteristics listed on which the teacher is to be judged are typically so general and undefined that two different principals rating the same teacher on the same characteristics can easily arrive at very different ratings. The characteristics are stated in such a way as to permit too many different interpretations. A second problem is that the characteristics (e.g., involvement with students, personal appearance and presence, extra curricular involvement, class presentations, organization) are only *indirectly* related to changes in the student. The assumption goes as follows: If the teacher rates high on most of these characteristics, he is no doubt bringing about desirable changes in the students. Thus, if a teacher's presentation appears clear and well organized (to the principal), the students are probably undergoing behavioral changes.

Since instructional objectives are statements of measurable student behaviors, they can serve as more direct evidence of teaching effectiveness. We can actually measure the degree to which desired changes in the student are being brought about; we do not have to make as many possibly erroneous assumptions such as the one above.

Both the principal and the teacher are typically dissatisfied with the principal's coming into the classroom several times a year and, after several hours of observation, filling out some rather cryptic forms which identify the teacher's "teaching effectiveness." This is not a secure position for either person. Would it not be safer and more thorough for the principal to obtain a list of the teacher's specific instructional objectives—which are open to far fewer interpretations—and with the teacher determine the degree to which the students have obtained the objectives? (This degree of attainment could be determined by taking student measurements of objective attainment over a period of time.)

If the objectives can be tied to the school's overall goals, and if the measurements show most of the students minimally mastering them, both the teacher and the principal can comfortably conclude that the teacher is doing an "effective" job of teaching. (By the same token, if instructional objectives can be used to designate effectiveness, can they also be used to identify ineffectiveness?)

Suggestions for the Teacher Emerging from This Area of Concern

1. Considering the present newness and unexplored areas in the field of instructional objectives, you should probably be somewhat discriminating in the extent to which you use them.
2. You should realize that instructional objectives will not solve all the problems that plague teaching; nonetheless, the advantages of using them far outweigh any disadvantages.

Area of Concern Six:
How Does the Use of Instructional Objectives Differ from What Teachers Have Been Doing All Along?

During the past several years, there has been such a preoccupation with learning how to define and write an instructional objective and how to differentiate it from a noninstructional objective, we have neglected to ask ourselves how this activity differs significantly from what has always occurred in education. Have teachers actually had and been using instructional objectives all along?

In looking at some possible differences between a teaching pattern which utilizes instructional objectives and one which is more typical in nature, we shall refer to Figure 2 below throughout the following discussion.

Figure 2. Teaching Patterns from a More Typical Approach and from an Instructional Objectives Approach

Pattern 1: A More Typical Teaching Pattern

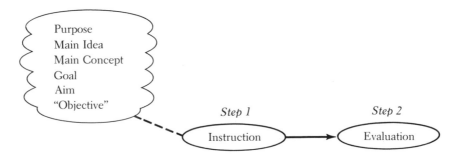

Pattern 2: Instructional Objectives Teaching Pattern

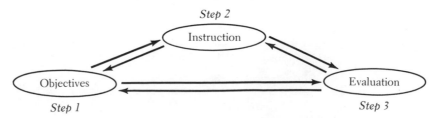

What Teachers Have Been Calling "Objectives"
Are Not Really Objectives

What have teachers been calling an "objective"? In order to obtain at least a partial answer, a great many lesson plans, district and school curriculum guides, teacher editions, and student texts were examined. Most of these contained sections entitled Purpose, Main Idea, Main Concept, Aim, Objective, or some combination of these. Such sections, whatever their titles, contained one of two things, either the topic to be taught or a teacher objective. According to the definition given in Area of Concern 1, an *objective* contains both the student's behavior and a topic; it does not contain the teacher's behavior or intentions. Therefore, based upon this definition, most of what is presented under titles such as those above does not qualify as an objective.

When a topic was stated in many of these sections, it was usually in the form of a conceptual statement, a simple concept, bits of information, a principle, or a generalization. Whichever form, the topic seldom contained any mention of the learner or his behavior; it was simply pure subject matter, free of any teacher or learner; it was that taught by the teacher to the student. Following are some examples of topics that appeared:

> The Family
> Families everywhere fulfill a few basic and significant functions although ways of living differ from society to society
> The earth and its features
> Gas expands when heated
> Quadratic equations
> Parts of a sewing machine
> Animals with fur coverings

Clearly, these are not objectives; they lack the learner and his behavior, and they are not consequences of the learning experience.

A second type of statement that appeared in these sections would be most appropriately called a teacher objective. These are statements about the teacher's intentions relative to some topic. Because they are about the teacher's behavior rather than the learner's, and because they identify experiences that are to take place rather than the consequences of these experiences, they do not qualify as objectives. Following are some examples of teacher objectives that appeared:

> To show reproduction of some of the five water colors of the past and present
> To develop an understanding of major rivers and mountains in the West (Note that this comes close to being a legitimate objective.)
> To expose students to the conditions that existed in the South prior to the Civil War

To conduct a mock trial
To visit the dairy
To explore the workings of a post office
To show how clay is thrown on a potter's wheel

These teacher objectives can be evaluated without even worrying about the student; with these statements, the teacher's behavior, not the student's, is really being evaluated.

Technically speaking, then, teachers have not had or used instructional objectives. This is one major difference between the two teaching patterns in Figure 2. In a typical teaching pattern, the teacher accepts topics and teacher objectives, along with a host of other things, as "objectives."

Using Instructional Objectives Places Greater Emphasis on Objectives and on a Clear Relationship Between Objectives and Instruction

In a typical teaching pattern (Pattern 1), a teacher's first *visible* step is the gathering of instructional materials and the planning of instruction. While objectives are no doubt "in mind," they are seldom written down as an initial activity. As such, instruction rather than objectives receives the greatest effort and concern. Thus, objectives are not allowed to provide any real directing power in developing instruction because they are either fuzzily located in the back of someone's mind or are not used at all preparatory to developing instruction. It follows that the relationship between objectives and instruction will be tenuous and difficult to tie down. Understandably, many teachers in this pattern do not see or feel the need for a clear relationship between the two, since their "objectives" have never been overly helpful in prescribing instruction anyway.

When instructional objectives are properly used (Pattern 2), the emphasis shifts from instruction back to the objectives. The majority of teacher time is spent generating both general and specific instructional objectives *rather than* gathering materials and planning instruction. Identification of objectives is the first step. Here the objectives play a major role in *prescribing* instructional experiences. Ideally, specific instructional implications flow easily from the objectives and do not require large amounts of teacher time. Here the relationship between objectives and instruction is mostly clear and very important.

Using Instructional Objectives Places Greater Emphasis on Evaluation and on a Clear Relationship Between Objectives and Evaluation

In the typical pattern of teaching, less emphasis is placed upon evaluation and more upon instruction, and there is little attention given to developing a clear relationship between objectives and evaluation.

More often than not, evaluation is that activity tacked on at the end of instruction for the major purpose of filling out grades. Someday, the reasoning goes, there will be no need for evaluation and grades; teachers can spend all of their time and energy on the more important calling of teaching. In the meantime, measuring instruments are those things used after instruction to determine how much the students have learned; they are not primarily for the modification of instruction. Both this misunderstanding of the purposes of evaluation and a lack of training in measurement principles have prevented teachers from seeing the important relationship between objectives and evaluation. Evidence of failing to emphasize this relationship can be seen in the painful consistency with which teachers construct and use invalid tests.

Using instructional objectives suggests a rather different emphasis. Evaluation becomes an integral part of the teaching act and is most crucial. The use of evaluation for grading is but one of its lesser functions. Far more important should be its use in providing feedback to instruction and objectives. Evaluation should provide information for making systematic changes in both the instruction and the objectives. Since evaluation plays this more enlarged role in teaching with objectives, its relationship to the objectives is important and needs to be clearly identified as much of the time as possible. When objectives become very specific (drill objectives) this relationship becomes so close that a one-to-one correspondence develops. That is, the objectives become virtually identical to the evaluation. With instructional objectives, on the other hand, the relationship cannot nor should it be that close because here the intent is to generate several *different* evaluation items, all of which measure the same objective.

Using Instructional Objectives Places Greater Emphasis on a Clear Interrelationship Between Objectives, Instruction, and Evaluation

Herein may lie the greatest difference between the two patterns of teaching. In the typical teaching pattern, since the relationship between all three elements (objectives, instruction, evaluation) is seldom clear or tied down, the elements themselves are not effectively used in providing helpful feedback to each other. That is, results from evaluation are not used to modify instruction because the former was not related to the latter in the first place. Furthermore, these results are of little help in altering the objectives if there is no clear relationship between objectives and evaluation. Such lack of feedback between the elements minimizes the making of systematic changes in teaching. On the other hand, if instructional objectives are conscientiously used, then there must be a clear relationship between the three elements. Objectives will provide clearer prescriptions for instruction and evaluation; evaluation, in turn, will provide clearer suggestions for instruction and objectives.

**Suggestions for the Teacher Emerging
from This Area of Concern**

1. In going through curriculum guides, textbooks, teacher editions, and other sources, you should not confuse such terms as Purpose, Aim, Main Idea, and Main Concept with legitimate objectives; in most cases, they are not.
2. Generally speaking, you should work out your objectives before designing your instruction so the former can be used to facilitate the latter.
3. You should continually strive to establish a reasonably clear relationship between objectives, instruction, and evaluation.
4. You should come to view evaluation as a crucial element of teaching with a variety of different uses, the most important of which is to provide suggestions for modifying instruction and objectives.

Area of Concern Seven:
How Useful Are General Educational Objectives?

Over the past several years as the instructional-objectives "movement" has begun to have an impact upon education, there has been an increasing tendency to criticize and reject general educational objectives. Many proselyters have argued rather persuasively about the meaningless-ness and nonmeasurability of traditional objectives found in education. As a result of this critical view, teachers now tend to shy away from general objectives and to concentrate only on more specific instructional objectives. To be sure, these large, educational objectives have been less than helpful, and their vulnerability has made them easy prey to virtually any critic; however, in our passion to rigorize education we may be overlooking their potential usefulness.

Teachers thinking up and writing down specific instructional objec-tives have, with uncomfortable frequency, emerged with rather dis-couraging results. All too often they end up with a set of unrelated and irrelevant drill objectives which are finally routed to the wastebasket. These trivial and unimpressive objectives can be attributed, in part, to the neglect of general objectives. Without more general guides, teachers have little or no systematic guidance in the generation of specific objectives, and they have no way to evaluate the importance of their objectives once generated.

The criticisms leveled against general educational objectives would be vastly minimized if these "objectives" were actually objectives. Many of them are simply phrases, general topics, or lone behaviors rather than legitimate objectives (refer back to Area of Concern 6). For example, if we converted the following:

> Learning how to learn
> Problem-solving skills
> Citizenship
> Growth in social skills
> Library skills
> Reading readiness

into legitimate objectives, their guidance in generating instructional objectives would be heightened. Thus, we would have:

> The student will have developed the *ability to learn* about new topics and acquire new skills in the areas of . . . .
>
> The student will be able to *solve problems* in the areas of city government and in . . . .
>
> The student will have become a better *citizen* on the playground and in the classroom.
>
> The student will have acquired new *social skills* in the following areas: . . . .
>
> The student will be able to demonstrate *library skills* each time he uses the library.
>
> The student will have developed *reading readiness skills.*

Following are some advantages of using these more general objectives:

1. General objectives provide guidelines for generating a group of related specific objectives.

2. General objectives can provide the relevance for specific instructional objectives. That is, the relevance of any specific (offspring) objective can be determined by tracing it back to its more general (parent) objective (see Figure 1, p. 13).

3. General objectives provide teachers with a more encompassing and complete picture of their efforts and thereby prevent them from unintentionally omitting desirable instructional objectives not readily apparent.

4. General objectives facilitate communication with nonprofessional people. Herein lies an interesting bit of irony. "Specific instructional objectives are important because they are communicable" was an original argument for their use. That is, two different people would come up with the same interpretation of a specific overt objective. Teachers and students, and teachers and other teachers, *do* tend to come up with similar interpretations of instructional objectives. However, when these specific objectives are presented to parents, school board members, and others who are unfamiliar with the language and the content in the classroom, they become less communicable. Nonprofessional people are more familiar with the words (behaviors and topics) used in general educational objectives than they are with those used in specific instructional objectives. Thus "The students will have developed an awareness of the World Wars" is more easily understood by them than "The students will be able to analyze the factors leading up to the outbreak of World War II and draw conclusions which would have alerted the United States to a potential air strike at Pearl Harbor."

In effect, we loosen the precision in order to increase the communicability between teachers and nonteachers. Ideally, perhaps, one would want specific instructional objectives that could be clearly communicated to nonprofessional people; but because of the variety of competencies and backgrounds represented outside of the classroom, more general objectives do tend to facilitate that communication. The author has had the experience of attempting to present rather specific objectives to people unfamiliar with the topics and behaviors in the objectives (e.g., district reading objectives to school board members). In order to receive at least some nod of understanding, the objectives had to be cast into more general and covert language. To be sure, it is important to state objectives in such a form so as to minimize alternative interpretations; however, it is also important to establish some communication in the first place.

5. The values of society and the community, as well as their priority, are more easily incorporated into general educational objectives than they are into specific instructional objectives.

Teachers generally have a difficult time explaining how the specific activities that go on in the classroom do in fact represent partial attainment of the values found in society at large. Although there are specific classroom objectives which do not easily lend themselves to any of society's values, there are a great many others which do. Further, most teachers no doubt feel some obligation to represent society's values in their classroom teaching. But to fit the values of society directly into specific classroom objectives is an unrealistic and most difficult task. First of all, these general values are often unwritten and diffused among the people in society. Second, even if they were written down, they would look very different from a teacher's instructional objectives. So what is to be done?

One possibility is to take smaller steps in incorporating values into objectives rather than one large jump. Stages are needed between a specific classroom objective and a value in society. Enter the general educational objective. Specific objectives can be visibly merged into increasingly more general objectives which begin to look more like some of the values in society.

To be sure, such a possibility is easier to think about than to implement, and teachers have not tried very diligently to build a visible ladder from specific objectives to values held by society. Since so few teachers have had any experience in doing so, clear and specific strategies are still unavailable. Even so, there is a significant need to give more serious attention to this task. For too long educators have avoided this responsibility. Even if a teacher succeeds in establishing a barely visible strand of connection between specific instructional objectives and some of society's values—through the vehicle of general educational objectives—that teacher will have made significant progress!

Society is becoming more and more involved in the educational priorities within the school system. More parents are becoming involved with the educational enterprise. This trend, along with that of increased accountability on the part of educators, strongly suggests that we spend more and greater effort attempting to incorporate the values of society into our statements of instructional objectives.

Quite often a school district will write down a statement of its philosophy, beliefs, or values. Since such statements are usually formulated by the combined efforts of teachers, administrators, school board members, and parents, they tend to reflect the feelings of society. Suppose these written statements were compared with a set of general educational objectives. What would be the difference between an objective and a value (or a philosophy or a need)?

Since teachers and curriculum planners have wrestled with this question to no small degree, perhaps some limited distinctions can be made. Distinctions between objectives and values are important because they eliminate confusion and because objectives turn out to be better prescribers of instruction than do values, philosophies, etc.

Simply put, any statement that does not contain the four characteristics described in Area of Concern 1 does not qualify as an objective. Typically, a philosophy, a value, and a need do not qualify. This can be observed from the following examples.

Philosophy: This is most often a group of belief statements put together into a unified document (sprinkled with plenty of beliefs, "oughts," and "shoulds"). Examples are as follows:

1. Children *should* have equal opportunity for schooling.
2. This district *is committed* to instructing the whole child.
3. We *ought* to teach for individual differences.
4. Children *should* experience "consciousness-raising" activities while in school.

Value: Functionally speaking, this is about like a philosophy. Examples are as follows:

5. Each child *should* progress at his own rate.
6. All children *should* have foreign language instruction.
7. All schooling *ought* to be coeducational.
8. Schools *ought* to instill in children the importance of work.

Need: This is typically a statement of deficit about which something ought to be done. Examples are as follows:

9. Children in the district *need* greater amounts of individualized help.
10. Teachers in the district *need* higher salaries.
11. The state's financial commitments *need* to be met in this district.

12. We *need* larger libraries.
13. Children *need* freedom for self-exploration.
14. Students *require* a variety of instructional opportunities.

The examples above can be contrasted with examples of corresponding educational objectives below.

3. Students *will have increased* their individual differences in the following areas: . . . .
6. Most of the children *will be able* to read and speak a foreign language.
7. The educational program *will have become* coeducational.
9. Students *will have received* more individualized help in the content areas.
10. Teachers in the district *will have obtained* higher salaries.
13. Children *will have become* more free to explore new areas of information.

It should be noted that values, philosophies, and needs are more often statements about what is to come or what is supposed to be; objectives, on the other hand, state what will have taken place or what will be the result. In addition, making an objective more general and inclusive does not make it any less of an objective. That is, a general objective does *not* turn into a value or philosophy just because it is made more general.

In conclusion, many of society's values can be transformed into general objectives and from there into more specific instructional objectives simply if people are encouraged to do so.

Suggestions for the Teacher Emerging from This Area of Concern

1. You should make a consistent attempt to incorporate the more general values of society into your specific instructional objectives through the use of general educational objectives made increasingly more specific.
2. You should, as much as possible, use general educational objectives as guidelines for generating specific instructional objectives.
3. You should not allow your educational objectives to be overly general; the prescriptive features of an objective become lost if this happens.
4. You should not mistake statements of philosophy, values, needs, etc., for objectives. Whatever the statement, if it does not contain the essential characteristics of an objective, then it cannot be called one.

Area of Concern Eight:
Have I Generated Measurable Objectives?

Problems with the Behavioral-Nonbehavioral Approach

Very few teachers and administrators by this time have escaped hearing statements like "Teachers should have behavioral objectives." This admonition, although having been uttered in different forms for many years, is presently the battle cry among many personnel in all phases of public education. Slogans such as "Down with nonbehavioral objectives" are very much on the scene. But suppose we ask this perfectly honest question, Why should we have *behavioral* objectives? A frequent response would be "If your objectives are behavioral, then you will be able to tell when they have been attained; not so with nonbehavioral objectives."

Such a reply suggests that behavior can be directly seen or heard; nonbehavior cannot. For example, *sharpening a pencil* is behavior and therefore can be directly observed. A behavioral objective would be "The student will be able to sharpen a pencil," because the teacher can actually observe a student sharpening a pencil and thereby tell whether this objective has been attained.

On the other hand, nonbehavior cannot be observed. *Understanding* is an example of nonbehavior. A nonbehavioral objective would be "The student will understand the mechanics of a pencil sharpener." There is no way to tell when this nonbehavioral objective has been attained.

How functional are these classifications? They are not very helpful for at least three reasons. First, to say that an objective is "nonbehavioral" does not tell us what it is, but only what it is not. It is not a behavioral objective. Second, we are mistakenly led to believe that all objectives fall neatly into one of these two categories. This is simply not the case. There are many objectives which are partly behavioral and others which are partly nonbehavioral. Third, a behavioral objective can quickly turn into a nonbehavioral objective, and vice versa. This double classification is most confusing to teachers and will be explained later.

The following is probably a more functional and realistic approach to take in considering the classification of objectives. First off, suppose we enlarge our definition of the term *behavior* to include not only observable activities but unobservable as well. Thus, *any* activity engaged in by the learner—observable or not—is a behavior. Since an objective must contain a behavior, all objectives are behavioral objectives.

How do behavioral objectives differ then? They differ in their degree of overtness, ranging from highly overt behavioral objectives to highly covert behavioral objectives. We can picture them as lying along a continuum from overt to covert. Thus when someone says, "I have a behavioral objective," the question might be asked, Is your behavioral objective mostly covert or mostly overt? Thinking of all objectives as behavioral objectives which differ in degree of observableness allows us to enlarge our thinking to include objectives occurring inside the learner as well as those we can observe on the outside. Also, we no longer need to assign objectives to unrealistic either-or classifications.

How can the remaining confusion, namely behavioral objectives turning into nonbehavioral objectives and vice versa, be handled? Here is how the problem arises. Suppose we are presented with a group of objectives and asked to identify them as either behavioral or nonbehavioral. Our decision is invariably based upon the verb in each objective. If the verb is an observable activity like *listing, writing, running,* or *reciting,* we conclude a behavioral objective. If, on the other hand, the verb is an unobservable activity such as *enjoying, thinking, evaluating,* or *appreciating,* we conclude a nonbehavioral objective. Why these conclusions? As a result of our reading, we have been led to believe that certain activities are always observable and others always unobservable. Thus, by simply looking at that activity in the objective we make a diagnosis.

Suppose one of the objectives we look at is "The student will be able to list the past three presidents of the United States." Since the activity *listing* has always been thought of as an observable activity, we designate this as a behavioral objective. But suppose the objective had appeared in a slightly modified form: "The student will be able to *mentally* list the past three presidents of the United States." Since we cannot observe a student mentally listing something, we suddenly have a nonbehavioral objective even though it contains the behavior *listing.* Such a confusion arises largely from classifying activities as always being either behaviors or nonbehaviors.

This confusion can be mostly eliminated by classifying *any* activity as a behavior which is more or less overt. Thus, *list* is a behavior in both of the above objectives. In the first it is mostly overt, and in the second, mostly covert. Now, rather than thinking there are behaviors and nonbehaviors and that a given activity is always one or the other, we can more easily think of every activity as behavior, with the particular context in which it is placed determining its degree of overtness. For example: "The student will mentally list . . . " (mostly covert), "The student will verbally list . . . " (mostly overt), "The student will feel a sense of appreciation for . . . " (mostly covert), or "The student will verbally express appreciation for . . ." (mostly overt.)

Finally, we can greatly minimize potential confusion simply by considering the entire objective rather than the behavior alone. Thus, an overt behavioral objective is so named because the entire objective appears overt rather than merely the behavior within the objective (see above examples).

We Measure Differences Between Behaviors

With this background, let us now return to the question, Have I generated measurable objectives? An overt behavioral objective is directly observable and therefore permits measurement. Since observable behavior is the only thing we can directly measure, overt behavioral objectives are necessary, not as ends in and of themselves but rather because they are measurable. The crucial concept is *measurability*.

What actually do we measure, and how is measurement related to objectives? Almost always, we measure differences between overt behaviors. There are at least three different measurements that can be made. First, we can measure the difference between a student's present overt behavior and some "ideal" overt behavior stated in an objective. This can be illustrated with a simple example. Suppose the objective is, "The student will be able to correctly sharpen a pencil." "Correctly sharpening a pencil" is a mostly overt behavior and represents our criterion, or ideal behavior. We hand the student a pencil and ask him to sharpen it. He goes up and tries to insert it into the wrong size hole and begins to crank the handle backwards. We directly observe this overt behavior which in this case constitutes our measurement. Our measurement tells us that there is considerable difference between the student's present overt behavior and that identified in the objective. He cannot sharpen a pencil.

A second measurement is the difference between a student's initial overt behavior and his changed overt behavior after instruction. We might join our frustrated student at the pencil sharpener and go through a series of demonstrations of correct pencil-sharpening behavior explaining each step as we go. After this, we might hand the student a second pencil and ask him to try it again. Now he easily inserts the pencil in the proper hole and smoothly turns the handle to produce a fine-pointed pencil. We measure the differences between his preinstruction behavior and his postinstruction behavior and conclude they are indeed different. (At this point we might also measure to see if his postinstruction behavior is finally comparable to the ideal behavior identified in the objective.)

A third measurement is the difference between one student's overt behavior and that of another. When working with objectives, we are usually less concerned with differences between students and more concerned with the above two measurements; nonetheless, this measurement has been widely used. Here is an example. Suppose both Stacy and Brett are presented with pencils and asked to sharpen them. Stacy jabs her pencil around in several different holes, finally inserting it into the proper one. Initially, she turns the handle backwards but then reverses it so that sharpening begins to take place. After some energetic starts and stops, she finally removes the pencil, which looks more like it has been chewed than sharpened. Brett, on the other hand, easily inserts his pencil into the proper hole and with consistent motion quickly produces a fine point. (He even blows the dust from the pencil.) Here we measure the difference between the pencil-sharpening behavior of Stacy when compared with that of Brett. Our conclusion is that Brett possesses more correct pencil-sharpening behavior than does Stacy.

It is obvious by now that an overt behavioral objective can be measured easily enough, but what about a covert behavioral objective? This cannot be measured. How can we tell whether or not it has been attained? With covert objectives, we must *infer* their attainment rather than measure it. Since a covert objective cannot be turned *into* an overt objective, it cannot *be made* measurable. What we can do, however, is substitute several overt objectives in its place, for these can be measured. If, through measurement, we determine that our substituted overt objectives have been attained, we should be willing to infer at least partial attainment of the covert objective. This is the only way we can "tell" whether or not a covert objective has been attained. (You might here review Area of Concern 3.)

Suggestions for the Teacher Emerging from This Area of Concern

1. You will experience less confusion if you think of *all* objectives as behavioral objectives which differ in their degree of overtness.
2. You should not think of objectives as being either covert or overt, but more or less of one or the other.
3. You should realize that the same behavior can appear mostly overt in one objective and mostly covert in another. A behavior is never always one or the other.
4. When determining whether an objective is mostly overt or mostly covert, you should consider the entire objective rather than merely the behavior within the objective.
5. You should refrain from viewing overt objectives as ends in themselves; they simply act as a means by which measurement can occur.
6. You should be more concerned about measuring the differences between a student's behavior and an "ideal" behavior stated in the objective, or between a student's behavior before instruction and after instruction; you should be less concerned about measuring differences between one student's behavior and another student's behavior.
7. You should remember that the attainment of overt behavioral objectives can be *measured* but that the attainment of covert behavioral objectives must be *inferred*.

Area of Concern Nine:
How Appropriate Are My Objectives?

The last area of concern was devoted exclusively to the question of the measurability of an objective. Quite a different question has to do with the appropriateness of an objective. We can take an educational objective and carefully generate from it a set of instructional objectives, all of which are specific and overt; however, they may also be trivial and unimportant!

In most workshops conducted by the author, teachers have at some point expressed disappointment with the notion of instructional objectives. Upon questioning, it has become apparent that dissatisfaction is not so much with an objective becoming measurable as with its appearing inappropriate. This continues to be a major concern for teachers.

There are two apparent reasons why teachers generate a high frequency of unimportant instructional objectives. First, as indicated earlier, they fail to start out with general educational objectives. These have been set aside or quietly forgotten in an attempt to deal only with measurable objectives. While there is still little information available on how these can be effectively used as guides in generating important instructional objectives, teachers who at least make an attempt to use educational objectives seem to end up with more worthwhile instructional objectives than teachers who start out and remain at a very specific level (refer to Area of Concern 7).

A second reason for an inordinate number of unimportant instructional objectives is simply inexperience in the whole business. Teachers attempting to generate instructional objectives for the first time quite naturally end up selecting only those that can be easily defined; initially, their main concern is with the measurability of whatever it is they construct. Time and energy usually run out before teachers can get very serious about the whole operation. Teachers with increasing experience in generating instructional objectives are able to come up with strikingly more appropriate instructional objectives than teachers with little or no experience. Thus, simply generating objectives over a longer period of time seems to improve a teacher's ability to come up with those which are more important. As teachers gain greater experience they become more imaginative in generating a variety of instructional objectives.

The question of whether we are talking about the appropriateness of educational objectives or instructional objectives might arise. This is rather difficult to answer for the following reasons. Suppose we think about a continuum of objectives ranging from educational down to specific drill objectives. At the one end almost all general educational objectives appear appropriate and important. Indeed, we seldom come across an educational objective which does *not* seem important. As we move along the continuum to objectives which are more specific and more overt (instructional objectives) and finally down to those which are highly limited (drill objectives), more and more of them appear unimportant or only marginally appropriate. This is probably because they are clear and specific; judgments about them can be easily made. For this reason, when we talk about the appropriateness of objectives, we will be referring to mostly instructional and drill objectives.

Following are some criteria that you, as a teacher, might use in determining whether or not your instructional objectives are appropriate. Perhaps this list will serve best if it triggers in your mind more specific criteria for your particular educational setting. Clearly, you would not want to invoke all these criteria for every instructional objective nor for that matter any particular one. Several might be used for deciding upon one objective, several more for another. Such factors as subject-matter area, age level of the students, institutional facilities, policies of the school, etc., will make some criteria more meaningful than others. The important point is that you use *some* clear and communicable criteria for deciding upon the appropriateness of your instructional objectives.

Criteria for Determining the Appropriateness of an Instructional Objective

1. Does the instructional objective seem relevant to the student? More and more teachers feel the responsibility to justify instructional outcomes to the student. Can the teacher provide the student with some reasons why the attainment of a given objective will be personally important to him?

2. Does the instructional objective itself provide any motivation for or is it at least attractive to the student? In the past, far too much of the student's motivation for learning has come from external sources such as teacher prodding through assignments and grades. We must somehow make the learning experience itself take on more attraction for the student. Perhaps presenting a clearer picture of the performance desired of the student will add some attraction.

3. Is the instructional objective appropriate for the needs of the student? Some students need certain types of objectives for emotional or psychological reasons. You might generate interpersonal objectives for withdrawn or insecure students or you might generate another remedial objective for students showing low achievement in a subject-matter area.

The point here is that some intellectual, emotional, or interpersonal need justifies the use of a particular instructional objective.

4. *Will the objective be used frequently enough by the student to make its attainment worthwhile?* This is a most important criterion because teachers will always be able to generate far more instructional objectives than can be attained by students within a given period of time. Many will have to be excluded. You may decide to retain one objective over another simply because the former would have wider use by the student.

5. *Can the instructional objective be attained by the student within the time alloted?* This is important because to embark on an instructional objective which cannot be attained until sometime after the teacher and student have separated does not allow the student or the teacher to be held accountable. The teacher cannot evaluate the degree of attainment of the objective and, therefore, cannot modify instruction or provide alternative routes for the student. But what if there is an important instructional objective which can be attained only over a long period of time? You might state it in such a way that a certain degree of its attainment can be achieved by the time the student leaves the class. Usually, extended objectives are educational objectives; for example, "The student will have learned to live in his society." As an offspring instructional objective at the first-grade level you might use "The student will be able to follow directions in cleaning up work areas." The instructional objective can be attained while both the teacher and the student are together, and it becomes partial attainment of the more long-term objective.

6. *Have each instructional objective's prerequisites been adequately attained?* Some instructional objectives are considered inappropriate because the student has not, as yet, reached a sufficient "readiness" level; that is, the objectives are premature. Since objectives will vary greatly in their number of prerequisites and since some will have few, if any, this criterion will be more useful in some content areas and at some levels than at others.

7. *Does the instructional objective specifically prescribe instructional materials and instructional experiences?* This is a most important criterion. The value of an instructional objective should show itself in these two areas. If the objective qualifies as an instructional objective, it will almost automatically tend to be prescriptive of instructional materials and experiences. For example, consider "The student will be able to identify those factors which contributed to the downfall of the Roman Empire within present American society." This objective provides at least some general prescriptions about teaching materials and experiences. The student would need exposure to the major aspects of Roman history and those factors leading up to its decline. Then the student would require some practice in identifying those same factors in present American

society. As a general rule, the more limited and overt the instructional objective, the more prescriptive it becomes.

8. *Are facilities available for the attainment of the instructional objective?* This is becoming an increasingly important criterion as teachers develop more ambitious and application-type instructional objectives. Also, there is movement toward the construction of facilities which foster greater individualization of instruction. Teachers within these settings are generating instructional objectives attainable only with a variety of materials and experiences. A problem arises, however, when teachers within a district are brought together to generate curriculum objectives for the entire district. Too often the newer schools possess facilities for implementation of the objectives while the older schools do not.

9. *Is the instructional objective important enough to justify the staff time and money put in for its attainment?* Here we must become involved with a cost-benefit decision. Some instructional objectives may be important and desirable, but not enough so to merit the time and expense required. For example, consider the objective, "The student will be able to correctly weigh materials that are less than one gram in weight." While this may be an important objective, the expense of buying sensitive scales and the time required for the instructor to teach their use may outweigh the importance of the goal.

10. *Can the instructional objective be modified or eliminated over time as it becomes more or less important?* Almost all instructional objectives will require modification from time to time as the values and emphasis of society change. This criterion becomes more important as schools make greater investments in hardware and facilities. Some objectives cannot be discarded simply because the school has purchased so much hardware for their attainment. For example, suppose society shifts emphasis from learning about planets and their relationships to earth to learning more about minority groups and relationships among people in large cities. A given school might be forced to retain interplanetary objectives simply because of its heavy investment in a planetarium!

11. *Can the instructional objective be evaluated satisfactorily?* Some objectives are selected over others simply because they are more easily and convincingly measured. Even though an objective's measurability is a completely separate dimension, it still becomes important in the area of appropriateness. If two objectives are of equal importance, then preference might be given to the more measurable one.

12. *Does a given instructional objective appear to be good evidence for the attainment of the educational objective?* This is a simple but important criterion. There are many instructional objectives generated from some educational objective which just do not seem to represent attainment of that objective. You might say, "I don't feel this particular instructional objective really does measure the student's appreciation of

literature, but I do feel better about this one. Also, I think other teachers would agree with me." This criterion might be labeled the "face-validity" test.

13. Is the instructional objective consistent with the teacher's own personal values? The influence of the teacher's value system upon the selection of instructional objectives is extremely powerful and should in no way be underestimated. No matter what guides you have before you and no matter what your responsibility, *you* have the final say about what will be appropriate objectives for your class.

14. Does the instructional objective appear to be consistent with the school's philosophy of education? As it turns out, a school's philosophy is usually so grandiose and inclusive, *any* instructional objective taught for can be easily construed as consistent with the school's philosophy. This criterion, however, will take on increasing importance in the future. Increasing pressure is being brought upon schools by board members and people in the community to sharply describe and significantly use school philosophy. In the future, school philosophies will be more clearly articulated so that some instructional objectives can be judged inappropriate. Suppose the following school philosophy: "We believe that the students in our school should be more directly exposed to the society in which they will live and function; that educational experience should be conducted as much as possible in the society itself and should be relevant to people living in the society." Although this is a rather broad and inclusive statement, it nevertheless provides some rough guidelines for making decisions about instructional objectives. For example, the following might be considered *in*appropriate by those in the school: "The student will be able to describe the general health conditions that existed in Europe prior to the outbreak of bubonic plague."

15. Is the instructional objective an "in-life" objective, or does it at least contribute to one? Teachers are generating more objectives which will have direct relevance to the student as he lives in society. Examples of "in-life" objectives are: "The student will be able to repair a car"; "The student will be able to enjoy a concert"; "The student will be able to make appropriate change from any cash sale"; "The student will be able to use a public library"; "The student will be able to vote correctly." Examples of objectives which do not have as close a tie to society are: "The student will be able to define various Latin words"; "The student will be able to diagram a sentence"; "The student will be able to solve quadratic equations with two unknowns"; "The student will be able to identify the major causes of the Civil War." (To be sure, these can have "in-life" relevance, but they are probably not as direct as the earlier examples.)

16. Is the instructional objective a prerequisite to later "in-school" objectives? If certain algebraic skills are prerequisite for calculus skills, which in turn are useful in understanding advanced statistical concepts, then instructional objectives in algebra are considered appropriate. Or, at a more specific level, suppose the following: "The student will be able to adequately play a chromatic scale on his clarinet." Certainly a prerequisite objective might be that he can "correctly mount a reed on the clarinet so that it will provide the greatest responsiveness to his lips." Reed mounting, then, would be considered an appropriate instructional objective. Or, if a student in art is intent on being "able to produce a pleasing pinch pot," an appropriate prerequisite objective might be "The student will be able to correctly throw clay on a wheel."

17. Is the instructional objective appropriate in terms of research results in learning? This criterion will undoubtedly take on greater importance as more human research is conducted in classroom-type settings. If research in areas like retention, transfer, concept attainment, maturational development, etc., suggests that a given instructional objective would be unlikely to be learned at certain age levels, then it would be an inappropriate objective for that age group. For example, suppose a kindergarten teacher has the following objective: "The students will have attained the concept 'strike' in baseball." Since this objective has a disjunctive conceptual rule and since research suggests that disjunctive concepts are not easily formed—especially in children this young—this would no doubt be considered an inappropriate objective.

18. Is the instructional objective too much like a drill objective? Many objectives are judged inappropriate by the teacher simply because they are too specific and too limiting. There is nothing wrong with teaching for a drill objective if indeed that is the teacher's intent. However, if the intent is to end up with an instructional objective but a teacher has produced a drill objective, then the latter is inappropriate for the purpose. Many drill objectives will appear more appropriate and satisfactory if they are converted into instructional objectives; this can be accomplished by rewording the drill objective so that it becomes slightly more inclusive and general. For example, suppose a teacher starts out with the following drill objective: "The student will be able to correctly set the clock hands at six o'clock." The teacher judges this to be mostly inappropriate because it is so limiting and rote in nature. With slight adjustment, however, it can be turned into a more satisfying instructional objective: "The student will be able to correctly place the hands of the clock at any setting specified by the teacher and will also be able to correctly identify any clock setting."

The above list of criteria for determining the appropriateness of an instructional objective is long and may have yet omitted other important criteria. You are encouraged to select and use only those which seem especially relevant for your particular situation. Whether from this list or your own, you should use some criteria. Judging the appropriateness of an objective actually requires more time and energy than does making it measurable. However, ending up with useful objectives is more than adequate compensation.

Suggestions for the Teacher Emerging
from This Area of Concern

1. The instructional objectives you generate should be appropriate as well as measurable.
2. You should devote as much or more time to an objective's appropriateness as to its measurability.
3. The appropriateness of any instructional objective should be determined by *some* criteria. You can select from the list presented herein or make up your own.
4. The likelihood of generating instructional objectives which are initially appropriate will be increased by (1) using educational objectives as guides and (2) keeping a large pool of possible topics and behaviors in full display during the generating activity.

Area of Concern Ten:
How Important Is It to Sequence Objectives in a Given Order?

As we study the great variety of literature that has been published in and related to the area of instructional objectives, we find a surprising absence of discussion about the ordering or sequencing of objectives. There has been considerable discussion about the use of taxonomies of educational objectives (e.g., the Bloom-Group Taxonomy), but careful scrutiny indicates that these taxonomies sequence only behaviors, not complete objectives. If the "cognitive" domain in the Bloom-Group Taxonomy is examined, for example, the sequence of behaviors is *knowledge, comprehension, application, analysis, synthesis,* and *evaluation.* Since these are behaviors, this is a taxonomy of behaviors rather than objectives. (For a more detailed discussion, see Area of Concern 15.)

But what about attempts to order subject matter or topics? Here, the situation is very different. The author conducted a survey to determine the degree of sequencing of subject matter in various subject-matter fields and across age levels. The sources for this survey were school, district, and state curriculum guides, teacher editions from a variety of publishers, student textbooks, a wide variety of local lesson plans used by teachers, and one review of subject matter being taught throughout the nation. This survey yielded several general observations:

1. Virtually every source sequenced each subject-matter area.
2. Sequencing was usually set up over all grade levels and also within each grade level.
3. There was considerable agreement among sources as to how certain subject-matter areas should be sequenced.
4. Very few sources had or had sequenced complete objectives; few if any student behaviors appeared in the earlier publications and not many more in the later ones.
5. Sequencing was more definite, extensive, and consistent in some subject-matter areas than in others. For some, only minimal sequencing occurred; for others, it occurred in great detail. Some were sequenced in a variety of ways while others were consistently

sequenced the same way. Subject-matter areas like math, the physical and biological sciences at the secondary level, reading at the elementary level, and foreign languages usually appeared in a rather definite and consistent sequence. On the other hand, subject-matter areas like social studies, physical education, art, and literature varied considerably in their sequences and degree of ordering.

Perhaps some tentative conclusions can be teased out of these observations.

1. Teachers, curriculum designers, and university professors have had considerable experience in sequencing subject-matter areas.
2. These people generally feel that, for some areas, one particular sequence is more conducive to learning than other sequences; for other areas, any number of different sequences will be equally effective in producing learning.
3. Most sequencing up to this point has been by subject matter, not by objectives.

In sum, we see that few people have been concerned with the sequencing of behaviors and a great many people concerned with the sequencing of subject matter. Very few people have made concerted attempts to sequence complete objectives (which include both behaviors and subject matter). An important question that needs to be studied in the near future is: To what extent should the sequencing of complete objectives be similar to the way we have sequenced behaviors and/or subject matter?

Let us turn directly to the question of sequencing instructional objectives. There seem to be at least two different situations in which teachers need to be concerned with the sequencing of objectives. In one situation, the teacher comes onto the scene, is handed a large group of objectives, and is asked to place them in a sequence for learning. Here, the teacher's task is mainly that of ordering and arranging the already constructed objectives. The second situation, which is probably more typical among teachers, is that of sequencing a set of objectives *while generating* them.

Regardless of the situation in which we find ourselves, we still must impose some sort of order or sequence upon the objectives for learning purposes. In deciding upon a given sequence, we should keep this question foremost in mind: In what sequence would these objectives be most easily learned by the greatest number of students?

Below are some suggestions about sequencing which have emerged from a variety of teaching workshops in which teachers have struggled with this very question. They also have arisen, in part, from the conclusions described above. They will serve as the suggestions emerging from this area of concern.

1. Placing objectives in a particular sequence is most important when the subject matter within the objectives requires a definite sequence (e.g., math or reading at the elementary level).

2. A number of different sequences may work equally well in more areas than teachers think.

3. There are at least two indicators teachers can use in deciding whether sequencing will be important:

   a. As the objectives to be learned become more complex, a particular sequence becomes increasingly important.
   b. As the age of the student decreases, the importance of a particular sequence increases.

There is some research which suggests that a given sequence is rather important if the student is learning very complex material, but that it is not so important if he is learning rather simple material. Also, younger students seem to require more careful sequencing than do older students. Teachers generating relatively simple objectives for older students do not need to be so concerned with sequencing. On the other hand, teachers who manufacture, say, reading objectives or math objectives, k through 6, must pay much closer attention to the question of a particular sequence. In either case, the teacher might well ask this question: Am I reasonably certain that these objectives will require a definite sequence for optimal learning?

4. If the objectives have already been constructed, they might be sequenced according to the difficulty of the entire objective, from easiest to most difficult. On the other hand, if the objectives are to be generated, the subject matter might be sequenced first by difficulty or by logical order. The resulting objectives would then be sequenced by difficulty of the subject matter. In the first situation, teachers work with the entire objective; in the second, only with the subject matter. Why not do it the same way in both situations? In the second situation, the teachers must start with something, and they have usually had the greatest experience in working with and organizing subject matter. Here they are very successful. Therefore, their past experience will help them most in the sequencing of subject matter. Once this has been done, they can go ahead and manufacture their objectives in that sequence. This is a much easier and more realistic task than attempting to sequence both the subject matter and the behaviors at the same time as the objectives are generated. Fortunately, both of the above procedures seem to produce rather similar results.

5. Whenever possible, teachers are encouraged to sequence objectives empirically, in terms of their difficulty. This means a teacher presents a class with several different sequences of the objectives and selects the sequence that best facilitates learning. One way to do this is to

gather information on how much difficulty the students have in achieving each objective and then order the objectives from least difficult to most difficult. The strength in this procedure is that the final sequencing of objectives is based upon the student's learning patterns, not upon the judgments of experts in the field (curriculum specialists or university professors writing textbooks).

6. Generally speaking, teachers should impose a sequence on the objectives *after* they have been generated, not before they are generated. Many teachers become bogged down in the unfruitful activity of using a taxonomy as a blueprint. "We will generate objectives at each level within the cognitive domain." With this procedure, the taxonomy rather than the teacher decides what kinds of objectives will be appropriate. All too often teachers end up with a large number of unwanted objectives for their particular age level and subject-matter area. A more pinpointed approach is to wait until after the objectives have been generated and then impose some structure or sequence upon them. This way you generate only those objectives which are of major importance to you.

This area of concern, as you can no doubt observe, will require greater attention by teachers and others who are interested in generating large sets of objectives for courses and entire curricula. Much progress is made simply by calling the teacher's attention to the task. Still, we need more information as to which subject-matter areas and skill areas will require careful sequencing and which will not.

Area of Concern Eleven:
How Are Objectives Used
in the Planning of Instruction?

Suppose after working through a manual entitled *How to Write Instructional Objectives,* a teacher comes away with these questions: What do I do now that I can write instructional objectives? Are they supposed to help me in my teaching? These telling questions suggest that we need to enlarge our focus from simply writing objectives to implementing them in teaching. Why has there not been a more systematic and convincing use of instructional objectives in the planning of instruction? There are several possible reasons.

First, teachers are just now reaching the point where they are ready to begin trying instructional objectives out in actual practice. For the last several years, most of the emphasis has been upon learning how to write an objective in behavioral terms, simply the acquisition of a mechanical-type skill. Attention is just now starting to turn toward the application of this skill in educational settings. A second reason has been the preoccupation with selling instructional objectives to teachers. The majority of articles, books, talks, workshops, and the like, have been more interested in telling teachers that instructional objectives are good things to have, and less interested in showing how they might be used. As a result, there are more arguments for and against having instructional objectives than there are suggestions for implementing them. The third and possibly most important reason has been that many objectives have been in a form which rendered them somewhat less than useful in the classroom. In bending over backwards to make all objectives specific, detailed, and overt, many teachers have made them nearly dysfunctional. Obtaining a behavioral objective has been more desirable than obtaining a useful one; as such, too many drill objectives have been manufactured. Since with drill objectives there is a nearly one-to-one correspondence between the objective and the instruction, these objectives have virtually become the instruction! Thus, attempting to prescribe instruction from a drill objective is like copying a sentence you have already written. Teachers have resisted this encumbering detail and inflexibility. They have played the game of writing objectives, but as for implementing them, that is something else. Time and experience should help minimize the foregoing objections; they are not serious and can be overcome in a relatively short period of time.

Let us return now to the original question: How are objectives used in the planning of instruction? This question would no doubt be considered the most important question in the book by many teachers. Two observations might be helpful at this point.

The first has to do with the overwhelming variation in the way teachers develop instruction for their students. Because teachers differ in their personalities, need systems, living styles, professional training, likes and dislikes, relationships with students, the type and age of students in their classes, and the subject matter they teach, they differ enormously in the way they prepare instruction. In view of these differences, there is little reason to believe they could be persuaded to use more standardized methods for developing instruction. If objectives are used to plan instruction, they will be used in an infinite number of *different* ways. For example, a teacher who prefers to be highly organized in lesson planning would probably use objectives to prescribe very specific and detailed instructional materials and experiences. Another teacher who feels repelled by organization, might use the same objectives as very rough guidelines. Yet another teacher, committed to total individualization, might use these objectives to prescribe a wide variety of different instructional experiences; a fourth teacher might use these objectives to prescribe but one type of instructional experience.

Thus, individual differences among teachers would cause them to use very different methods for prescribing instruction from objectives. Presumably, teachers will use objectives in ways which are conducive to their own personal teaching styles. In light of this, how useful would it be to have a specific method for using objectives to prescribe instruction?

A second observation concerns the question itself: How are objectives used in the planning of instruction? Evidence from various workshops suggests that if teachers generate instructional objectives (rather than drill objectives), the question seldom arises! Teachers simply go ahead and develop appropriate instruction on their own. The crucial step does *not* seem to be the developing of instruction; rather, it is the generating of instructional objectives. Teachers seldom have difficulty deciding upon materials or developing lesson plans once they have functional objectives. If appropriate sources are available, teachers move through them quickly and easily, experiencing little trouble selecting relevant activities for the student, visual aids, discussions, etc. There seems to be a very important relationship between the form of the objectives (educational, instructional, drill) and the ease with which instruction can be developed from them. Teachers—especially those with more experience—typically come to the task of developing objectives having had considerable practice and experience in selecting and developing instructional materials and activities. Objectives, when stated in a functional form, do nothing more than facilitate this process. Many teachers have been asked how they go about deriving instruction from their objectives; they report a variety of methods used, some of which they are unable to verbalize. But most of these methods seem to get the job done with relative ease and satisfaction. Teachers are consistent in reporting that moderately specific objectives facilitate their efforts.

In using your own method, you might consider two more general orientations which help guard against the selection of inappropriate instructional experiences.

Orientation 1: Objectives Should Be Thought of as Prescribers of Instruction Rather Than as Fallouts from Instruction

Most of us at one time or another have been handed a written prescription from our doctor which, when presented to the pharmacist, directs him to provide us with some medication for our ailment. This slip of paper tells the pharmacist what to prepare, how to prepare it, and in what amount. It is very directive in nature. A prescription does more than simply describe the medicine; it directs us how to use it. To prescribe is to guide or direct. Objectives, if they are to be of significant value, need to be prescriptive in nature. Though most objectives are not as rigorously directive as a doctor's prescription, they need to act as *guides* in directing teachers to appropriate materials and instructional experiences. Herein lies their power.

Objectives possess most of their power if generated *prior* to instruction. If they have to be continually teased out of already-existing instruction, their directing power is unused. Shaking a group of objectives out of some instruction solely for the purpose of having a set of objectives is nothing more than an intellectual exercise. To be sure, a beginning teacher or one involved for the first time in a new unit may need to use existing lesson plans and textbooks initially, but from then on, the objectives should be in the driver's seat as much as possible.

As we contemplate the prescriptive nature of objectives, we might note the relationship between the form of the objective and its prescriptiveness. An educational objective has little prescriptiveness about it; by comparison to other forms, it provides only general guidelines. But, as an objective becomes more specific and more overt until it qualifies as an instructional objective, its prescriptiveness increases. That is, instructional objectives provide much more specific guidelines. Finally, as the objective becomes specific enough to qualify as a drill objective, it becomes prescriptive to the point where it identifies the exact instruction, no more and no less. Drill objectives, in a real sense, become the precise lesson plan for the teacher and the exact study guide for the student (similar to the doctor's prescription for the pharmacist). A one-to-one correspondence exists between the objective and the instruction.

The problem with overly prescriptive objectives is that they provide no breathing room for either teachers or students. The instruction must come out of each student in exactly the same form it went in. With instructional objectives, on the other hand, teachers are allowed variation in their instruction, and students in their behavior. Finally, as we move back up to very general objectives, we find that they provide so little direction that any number of materials and instructional experiences can be accommodated and considered as appropriate.

This discussion has implications for various groups generating objectives for curriculum purposes. If the objectives are being generated by a group of teachers and curriculum specialists for district-wide use, they should be left general enough so they can prescribe a variety of different materials and instructional experiences to satisfy different teachers and students. If, on the other hand, objectives are being generated by a single teacher for a group of thirty students, they can become somewhat more specific, and thereby prescribe more directly the appropriate materials and experiences. The more prescriptive these objectives become, the more easily the teacher can make decisions about which materials and experiences are appropriate and which are not; at the same time, however, fewer materials and experiences will turn out to be appropriate in teaching for those objectives which are more prescriptive.

Orientation 2: Attempts Should Be Made to Develop "Valid" Instruction

This second orientation asks us to be more concerned with the relationship between instruction and objectives: Is the instruction generally valid in terms of the objectives?

The term *validity* will be discussed in greater detail in Area of Concern 12; here it will be described only briefly. All of us are no doubt familiar with this statement: A test is valid if it measures what it is supposed to measure. Very simply, this means that when we design a test to measure our objectives, it should call forth the same behaviors and content that are identified in the objectives; there is a high correspondence between what is found in the objective and what is found in the test. A high correspondence means that the test is mostly valid in measuring the objectives.

The same concept might be used in thinking about the correspondence between our objectives and our instruction. Loosely speaking, is there a high correspondence between what is covered in the instruction and what is covered in the objectives? More precisely, are the topics covered in the instruction and the behaviors we have the student perform similar to the topics and behaviors in the objectives? If so, we can say the instruction is "valid." A note of caution should be voiced here. If the correspondence between the objectives and the instruction is perfect;

that is, if the objectives are identical to the instruction, we find ourselves in the old trap of ending up with drill objectives. In most cases, teachers would feel uncomfortable with such a tight and direct correspondence between objectives and instruction. But suppose the opposite extreme. Suppose there was absolutely no correspondence between the objectives and the instruction! Either extreme is to be avoided.

Simply asking teachers to think about the "validity" of their instruction or to think in terms of a rough correspondence between instruction and objectives has produced satisfying results. In the process of developing instruction from a set of objectives, if a teacher continues to ask, Is this material relevant to my objectives? that teacher usually comes up with rather appropriate instruction.

A relationship exists between orientation 1 and orientation 2. If an objective is very prescriptive in nature, then the validity of any instruction designed for that objective can be easily determined. Thus, as prescriptiveness increases, the validity of instruction can be more easily determined. Since an educational objective is so lacking in prescriptiveness, the validity of any selected instructional experience is more difficult to determine. If we have a drill objective which is very prescriptive in nature, the validity of an instructional experience can be easily ascertained. For example, suppose the educational objective, "The student will become aware of his environment." What instructional materials and experiences would be valid? Which ones would be invalid? It would be difficult to tell. Since the objective has so little prescriptiveness, it would be difficult to reject any experience as being invalid. But consider the following drill objective: "The student will be able to name the three mountains surrounding his community." This is very prescriptive. Obviously, we would not show the student pictures of major lakes and rivers in his state; nor would we tell him about the various ores found in the mountains nearby. Both of these would be less valid experiences for this particular objective.

The two orientations presented here should be used regardless of the methods teachers use in developing instruction from objectives. They are safeguards to be kept in mind with any strategy for they help teachers to derive instruction from prescriptive instructional objectives rather than from some undefinable source.

Suggestions for the Teacher Emerging from This Area of Concern

1. You should use instructional objectives prescriptively to suggest instructional materials and experiences.

2. If you continually work at casting your objectives in the appropriate form (generally, instructional), you will have little difficulty in developing appropriate instruction.
3. You are encouraged to use any method that works for you as you use objectives to prescribe instruction.
4. You should continually ask the question, Is my instruction valid in terms of my objectives?

Area of Concern Twelve:
How Can I Tell When My Objectives Have Been Attained?

Differences Between Measurement and Evaluation

Generally speaking, the discussion so far has revolved around the generating of instructional objectives and their use in prescribing instructional experiences. In the minds of many, these are the two paramount steps in the process of teaching, and from here on the teacher simply carries out the actual instruction. If we were to stop at this point, however, virtually all of the foregoing discussion would be in vain. To be sure, we can generate objectives, plan and conduct instruction, and then stop; but the minute we look back, raising the question of how we might improve our instruction, or whether our teaching has been "effective," another element must be added—that of evaluation. If we fail to conduct at least minimal evaluation, there will be no way of knowing whether or not objectives have been attained by the students, or the degree to which instruction has been effective in their attainment. Without feedback through evaluation, how can we tell whether or not changes have occurred?

Suppose a randomly selected sample of one thousand teachers were asked the question, Do you consider evaluation to be important in teaching? All one thousand would no doubt respond with an emphatic "Yes!" Few would disagree that evaluation is important in teaching. But disagreement would begin to arise about the *kind* and *extent* of evaluation in teaching. When teachers are asked, How do you evaluate your students? or, To what extent do you think evaluation should occur? or, What kinds of evaluation instruments should a teacher use? considerable differences of opinion arise. Some teachers strongly believe that a student's performance should be evaluated totally by subjective judgment; other teachers believe with equal conviction that evaluation should be based upon results of "objective" measuring instruments and only after considerable measurement has occurred. Further, some teachers consider the use of paper-and-pencil tests to be a weak and inappropriate method for evaluating students, while others rely almost entirely upon them. Finally, some teachers believe strongly in evaluating certain kinds of student objectives and not others. Some would evaluate computational skills in math and knowledge of biology while at the same time refuse to evaluate other kinds of student objectives like attitudes toward learning, appreciation of others, and emotional adjustment. Thus while most teachers agree that evaluation should occur in teaching, they disagree about what should be evaluated, how it should be evaluated, and the extent to which evaluation should take place.

At this point it might be useful to distinguish between two terms: measurement and evaluation. *Measurement* refers to the rather limited activity of gathering and quantifying information. No inferences, interpretations, judgments, or decisions are made about the information. This information is gathered and classified through the use of a *measuring instrument*. This instrument can be virtually anything that collects raw data, be it observation by the teacher, a true-false test, a rating scale, an attitude scale, a personality inventory, an I.Q. test, or an anecdotal record kept by the teacher.

Often the students are the ones who use the measuring instrument. They might fill out a questionnaire, an interest inventory, or work through a multiple-choice test or complete an essay question. In other situations, the teachers use the measuring instrument. They might use a checklist to determine a student's tidiness in clearing up his desk; or a rating scale to measure his attitude toward playground activities; or an anecdotal record to keep track of his progress in manipulative skills.

It is important that we remember *not to limit* our views of measuring instruments to the more commonly used paper-and-pencil tests; we need to keep our views inclusive. The problem with a restrictive view of a measuring instrument is that there will also tend to be a restrictive view of the types of objectives that are possible to generate. Thus only those objectives that lend themselves to easy paper-and-pencil measurement will tend to be generated. Rather than omit important but difficult-to-measure objectives, we are charged with the responsibility of constructing our own appropriate measuring instruments. This will keep us from falling into the common trap of allowing the tail (measuring instrument) to wag the dog (objectives).

Measurement is just one activity in the more general process of evaluation. *Evaluation* not only includes measurement but also the making of judgments and decisions based upon the gathered information. It is in evaluation, not measurement, that our experience, judgment, and intuition predominantly enter the picture.

How can a distinction between these two activities be helpful in our discussion? As was suggested earlier, almost all teachers use evaluation in their teaching; not all of them use measurement, and many of those who do, fail to use it carefully. There are two major suggestions upon which the following sections will be based. First, teachers need to engage in more measurement as they evaluate. Second, this measurement needs to be more systematic and rigorously conducted. If more and better measurement is conducted by teachers, then overall evaluation will be more accurate and sound. In the discussions that follow, there is no intention to lessen the importance of judgment and experience in the overall process of evaluation; nor will we suggest that evaluation be based solely upon measurement alone. Rather, teachers who improve the quality and extent of their measurement will improve the quality of their judgment and hence their evaluation.

Indeed the majority of problems encountered by teachers as they evaluate can be directly linked to the quality and extent of their measurement. Inadequate evaluations are usually based upon faulty measurement or, in more extreme cases, upon little or no measurement! Though measurement is only one phase of the evaluation process, it is the basis from which the other phases stem; as such, this area of concern will be limited to the improvement of measurement procedures.

Desirable Characteristics of Any Measuring Instrument

A Measuring Instrument Should Be Valid
for the Objectives It Measures

When you administer a measuring instrument to your class, you obtain a set of scores; these scores should be a valid measure of your objectives. Let us examine this more closely, recalling that an objective contains both a behavior and a topic. If a measuring instrument calls forth the same (or nearly the same) behaviors and topics that are identified in the objectives, then the scores are said to be *valid*. Or, less precisely, the instrument is said to be valid. On the other hand, if the measuring instrument calls forth behaviors and content which are rather different from those identified in the objectives, then the results are said to be mostly *invalid*. Stated in a slightly different way, an objective asks the student to demonstrate some behavior relative to some content; a measuring instrument also asks the student to demonstrate some behavior relative to some content. The degree to which the two behaviors and the two topics correspond will be the degree to which the instrument is valid. Suppose we examine several examples.

Objective: The student will be able to define photosynthesis.

Measuring instruments: 1. Define photosynthesis.
2. Chlorophyll is affected by water. (*T-F*)
3. Draw a picture of a plant growing out of the ground.

Measuring instrument 1 is valid because the behavior called forth in the instrument is identical to the behavior ("define") identified in the objective. Additionally, the topic called forth in the instrument is identical to the topic ("photosynthesis") identified in the objective. Measuring instrument 2 is less valid because the instrument is asking the student to judge the truth or falsity of a statement, and that is really a different behavior than "defining." Also, the instrument is asking about only a small part of the topic identified in the objective. Measuring instrument 3 is completely invalid because "defining" and "drawing" are very different behaviors and also because a plant simply growing out of the ground is rather far removed from the process of photosynthesis.

The above objective, chosen for illustration, is simple and uncomplicated. As a result, the relative validities of the three measuring instruments can be easily judged. Most of the time, however, objectives are more complex and less clear-cut, which makes decisions about the validity of any given measuring instrument more difficult. That is, as an objective becomes somewhat more general, several different measuring instruments might be valid for the objective—for example, "The student will be able to correctly tell time." What would be valid measures of this objective? We might give the student a picture of a clock setting and ask him to *identify* the correct time. Or we might present him with a clock which has movable hands and ask him to *place the hands* at the proper setting when given various times. Or we might even ask him to *explain* the relationship between the small hand and the large hand of a clock. Each of these measurés asks the student to perform somewhat different behaviors and, to some extent, the topics vary. Are they all valid measures? What is the relationship between their behaviors and that identified in the objective? What is the relationship between topics? We can observe that the validity of these instruments is slightly more difficult to discern because the behavior in the objective is not overly precise. Yet most teachers would accept these as generally valid instruments. There does appear to be a reasonable relationship between the behaviors and the topics in each.

The above type of validity is called "content" or "logical" validity. Teachers must discern the validity of a given measuring instrument through logic and judgment. They need simply ask themselves, Is there a reasonably good relationship between the behaviors called forth in the test and those identified in the objectives? (Is the learner doing about the same thing in both cases?) Is there a reasonably close relationship between topics? With minimal practice, teachers are able to become rather skillful in judging the content validity of their evaluation instruments. Of all the desirable characteristics of a measuring instrument, content validity is most important and should be conscientiously worked for by teachers. If a measuring instrument generally fails to measure what it has been designed to measure, all other characteristics lose their meaningfulness. How do teachers ensure adequate validity in their measuring instruments? Chiefly by making certain their objectives are clearly defined, for the objectives provide the standards for making judgments about the validity of the measuring instruments; the sharper the standards (objectives), the more accurate the judgments about the degree of relationship between the objectives and the measuring instruments.

A Measuring Instrument Should Have
at Least Some Consistency
in Measuring Whatever It Measures

Imagine the following situation. You construct a multiple-choice test designed to measure a group of objectives. You administer the test on Monday and the same test again on Tuesday. Since only twenty-four hours have passed between the first and second testings, you would expect the student rankings on both tests to be about the same. For example, if John, Mary, Claire, and Sue obtained the four top ranks and Stan, Ruby, Shanna, and Charles obtained the four bottom ranks on Monday, you would expect about the same rankings just twenty-four hours later. You would certainly not expect Stan, Ruby, Shanna, and Charles to be among the top ranks on Tuesday. If the rankings are about the same on Tuesday as they were on Monday, you have some evidence that the test is consistent in its measuring. The results from such a test are *reliable* results.

But what if the results from the test are very unreliable? This means the test is inconsistent in ranking people. Suppose that John ranked first one day and third from the bottom on the next day, while Charles changed from lowest rank to third rank, and so on. How much confidence could you place in any given score? If your results are unreliable, you must become distrustful of any obtained score. John's score of 72 may not even approximate his "true" score. If you had him work through the same test again, he might receive a score of 60. Thus, unreliable measuring instruments cause scores to be too inconsistent. When the reliability of a test is too low, it cannot be a highly valid test.

There are other reasons why it is important to work for reliable measuring instruments. Suppose on the first day of class you give your students a test carefully designed to measure your objectives. You are interested in finding out what percentage of the students can already master the objectives prior to instruction; also, you are interested in measuring the effectiveness of your instruction. After instruction takes place, you readminister the same test to your students. If your instruction has been effective, you would expect the class average to be higher on the second testing than on the first. Suppose the mean on the test is in fact eight points higher at the end of instruction. If the test turns out to be rather inconsistent (unreliable) in its measurement, you could not tell whether this difference was due to the instruction or to the unreliability of the instrument. Surely you would not want to pat yourself on the back for good teaching if most of that difference were due to nothing more than a poorly constructed measuring instrument. In this case, high reliability allows you to make more confident judgments about the effectiveness of your instruction.

Suppose you do not give a test on the first day of class, but only at the end, after your instruction. Do you still need to worry about the question of consistency of your measuring instrument if it is given only once? Yes, but for different reasons. In the above situation you needed to make confident judgments about the effectiveness of your instruction; here you need to make confident judgments about the degree to which your students have attained their objectives. Suppose your instrument tells you that John has barely failed to master the objectives; but he did come close. If you readminister the same test, John might now attain a slightly higher score showing mastery of the objectives. Thus, even a single testing must produce results which are somewhat reliable in order to make confident judgments about an individual's score.

At least one way to improve the reliability of a measuring instrument used to measure objectives (as compared to being used to determine relative standing in the class) is to increase the number of items or questions in the instrument. More items provide a better picture of a student's true achievement of the objectives.

All measuring instruments used by teachers should have some validity and reliability. This applies to instruments like true-false tests, multiple-choice tests, short-answer and essay tests, questionnaires passed out to the students, checklists used by the teachers, attitude scales, personality inventories, measures of manual skills, and so on. For this reason, when talking about measuring instruments, we need not make major distinctions among those measuring intellectual objectives, affective objectives, (e.g., attitudes, feelings, values), and motor objectives (e.g., running, sewing a dress, executing a block).

Constructing a Measuring Instrument

Suppose we go through the process of constructing a measuring instrument for a set of instructional objectives. Among other things, we want the instrument to have respectable validity and reliability.

Suppose for a given unit we have generated ten instructional objectives which are all cognitive in nature. First off, we might go through these objectives and underline the behavior in each. Then we would decide upon the most valid type of measuring instrument for each objective. For each we would ask, What type of instrument will call forth behaviors similar to those underlined? For one objective, for example, we might ask, What kind of instrument will ask the student to "describe"? In this particular case a short-answer question would work well; after studying the other nine objectives, we might decide that five are best measured by short-answer items and four by matching items.

Next, we would start manufacturing the items. If all ten objectives are to be given equal weight, then each objective should have about the same number of items. We would try to generate a minimum of at least three items for each objective. The more different (though still valid) the items that can be constructed for an objective, the higher will be the reliability of the measuring instrument. In constructing the items for a given objective, care should be taken to make certain that the topic and the behavior in the item are related to the topic and the behavior in the objective. (Once conscious of this requirement, teachers have little trouble constructing valid measuring instruments.)

Suppose we are able to construct five items for each of the ten objectives. Let us examine the five items for objective 1. These five vary in difficulty. Some are rather easy and others more difficult. This prevents developing a test which does nothing more than discriminate among students. An easy item is one that is passed by a large percentage of the class; a difficult item is passed by only a small percentage of the class. Items measuring each of the other objectives also vary in their difficulty.

Again let us look at the five items measuring objective 1. Each individual item should be working effectively. This means that if the students have mastered objective 1, they will tend to pass the item, but if not, they will tend to fail it. This should be the characteristic of each of the other four items measuring objective 1, and for those measuring the other objectives. There is a simple method we can use to determine whether or not an individual item is working effectively. The item can be administered to the class before instruction and after instruction. If a higher percentage of the students pass the item after instruction than before instruction, the item is working with some effectiveness. Thus, if 20% of the class pass the item before instruction and 60% pass it after instruction, the item is generally doing its job.

In order to use this method, we must be able to score an item as either "pass" or "fail." There is no problem with a true-false item and neither is there with a multiple-choice item because with each the correct alternative can be thought of as "pass" and all the incorrect alternatives as "fail." With short-answer and essay items, however, some adjustment must be made. Suppose there are 10 points possible on a given essay item; we could say that if a student achieves from 1 to 4 points he fails the item, and if he achieves from 5 to 10 points he passes the item. Thus most items can be considered on a pass-fail basis.

We now end up with a fifty-item test measuring the ten objectives. Each objective is measured by five different items which vary in difficulty; each item is working with some effectiveness. Keeping a close eye on each objective as we generated its five items has helped us build content validity; attempting to include as many different items (still valid) for the time allowed has helped build some reliability. Finally, within the test, we group those items measuring each objective; this is done so that we might identify those objectives with which students have trouble.

How Do We Measure an Objective?

Student Performance Compared with Some "Ideal" Performance

What is meant by "measuring" an objective? One type of measurement is done by measuring the degree to which a student has attained some objective. More specifically, this entails measuring the degree to which the student's behavior in some subject matter *approximates* the "ideal" behavior directed at some content, which we call an objective; we ask to what degree the student finally approximates the objective. A first thought might be that this measurement occurs only at the end of instruction. However, a teacher could measure this degree of approximation any time during the learning experience or at its end. The teacher's main concern, however, is not with student growth over a period of time, but rather with the degree to which each student finally approximates the objective. This may occur immediately or after an extended period of time.

Student Performance Before Instruction
Compared with Performance After Instruction
    A different but equally important type of measurement is done by measuring the degree of change in students over a period of time, usually from the outset of instruction to its completion. Here the interest is not so much in how closely students approximate the ideal at the end, but rather in the amount of growth each has achieved during the process: At the end of instruction a student may yet fall short of the ideal in the objective but, at the same time, have shown considerable growth. In a typical setting, a teacher will administer a measurement before beginning instruction (sometimes called preassessment or pretest) and also after instruction (postassessment or posttest). The difference between a student's pretest score and posttest score constitutes the amount of gain.

    Suppose, for discussion, we call these two measurements of interest the "ideal" model of measurement and the "pre-post" model of measurement. Both have advantages and disadvantages. An advantage in using the ideal model is that it fits more comfortably with the whole notion of instructional objectives. Here, perhaps, teachers are more ambitious in desiring their students to reach a certain level, being less content with merely growth in that direction. A second and possibly more important advantage of the ideal measurement model is that students need not be subjected to a preassessment, which they all too often fail. A disadvantage with this model is that it does not provide teachers with the students' levels of competence prior to instruction; they might be able to achieve the objective already. In such cases, why bother with instruction? Also, if teachers lack experience in making sound judgments about abilities, they may place undue and unnecessary pressure upon students to achieve certain levels.

    The pre-post measurement model has the advantage of providing some "baseline" performances on students. With this model, teachers are able to determine whether or not the students can already demonstrate the attainment of an objective. Secondly, this model gives teachers more information about the effectiveness of their instruction. If there are no gains between the pre and posttesting, the instruction needs modification or perhaps complete revision.

There are disadvantages with the pre-post measurement model, however. Ideally, the pre and posttesting should be "parallel" in what they measure. This is a rather difficult state to achieve. If the tests are measuring different behaviors and topics, then differences between the pre and posttesting can be as likely attributed to different tests as to the instruction. Even if the same test is used for both the pre and posttesting, there is still the problem of unreliability. Many teacher-made tests suffer from being inconsistent in measuring. As such, any gain score will reflect some unreliability of the measuring instrument. A further disadvantage has to do with the time between pretesting and the onset of instruction. Of what help is it to know that the students can already attain the objective if the pretest is administered on the opening day of class? Teachers would have difficulty revamping or individualizing their objectives there on the spot.

Perhaps some compromise between the two models could combine the advantages of each. Rather than administering a complete and comprehensive pretest, you could simply sit down with your students and ask several questions which could be answered if the objectives were already attained. On the basis of student response, you would be able to make a rather accurate judgment about the degree to which the objectives have already been achieved. If the students appear to be in command of them, they would go directly to the posttest, bypassing instruction. On the other hand, if you remain unconvinced, you may have the students go through the instruction. This "mini" preassessment, though less reliable, takes very little time, does not labor the students, and usually provides enough information to make a reasonably sound judgment.

What Constitutes "Mastery" of an Objective?

Deciding upon a Mastery Level

Suppose we have one objective and have designed a measuring instrument for it which includes every possible item *that can be* manufactured as a measure of this objective. Certainly we should be able to say that if a student correctly answers all the items in this population he has mastered the objective. But obviously, no teacher can or should manufacture all possible items for one objective; to attempt such a feat is unnecessary and a waste of time. In reality, teachers simply develop a sample of items from the population. They are willing to assume that the students will perform on the sample in much the same way they would perform on the entire population. Thus they allow performance on the sample to *stand for* performance on the population. If a student correctly answers 90% of the questions in the sample, he could probably correctly answer about 90% of the questions in the entire population. On the other hand, if a student correctly answers only 10% of the items in the sample, he could probably correctly answer only about 10% of the entire population.

As teachers, we make an inference about how our students would perform with the population by knowing how they perform with the sample. Since this inference is made, it becomes very important that the sample of items we develop are representative of the population of items that could be developed. The extent to which we attempt to do this is the extent to which we can feel comfortable about making an inference to the population of items.

Now that we have determined the need for a representative sample of items measuring the attainment of an objective, how do we determine the point at which mastery can be assumed? The decision about what constitutes mastery has to be *arbitrarily made* by the teacher. Certainly we would want to make certain that our level of mastery is above a score that could be obtained by chance alone. If a test contained twelve true-false items, a student could obtain a score of six (50%) by chance alone. Whatever percentage you select to constitute mastery, you should have some reasons for your selection. You may, for example, decide that 90% (a score of eleven) will constitute mastery because the items are rather easy, because the chance score is rather high (50%), and because the material itself is very important as a foundation for future learning.

Following are some guidelines suggested by Millman (1970), Crawford (1970), and others that might be considered in setting a mastery level:

1. Some objectives by their very nature will require a perfect or near perfect mastery. Here is an extreme example: "A pilot will be able to perform correct landing operations when landing at O'Hare Airport." The consequences of anything less than perfection or complete mastery with this objective are disastrous. In a less spectacular vein, "The student will have correctly memorized all of the multiplication tables from one through ten," requires complete mastery. If the student plans to go into engineering, the consequences of not attaining complete mastery of this objective may be likewise unfortunate. At the same time, there are other objectives which by their very nature do not require near or perfect mastery—for example, P.E. objectives. "The student will be able to perform fifty sit-ups." If he cannot perform all fifty, the consequences are not nearly as disastrous. Or "The student will follow correct cooking procedures in baking brown bread." Perhaps the most devastating consequence of less than perfect mastery here would be a rather disgruntled spouse. Thus, the consequences that can result from non-mastery should determine how stringent a teacher must be. Correctly answering 50 to 70% of the items may constitute mastery if the consequences of nonmastery are not crucial. On the other hand, 90% or above

might constitute mastery if the consequences of nonmastery are very crucial.

2. If the objective to be attained is important for future in-school learning, then mastery should be set at a higher level than if the objective is not tied to later learning. For example, near perfect mastery of the periodic table would be required for any student studying for advanced chemistry.

3. If the items are such that a student can attain a rather high score by guessing alone, then mastery should be set at a higher level. Mastery for true-false items would need to be higher than mastery for multiple-choice items because the student would tend to correctly guess about 50% of the true-false items but only about 25% of the multiple-choice items.

4. If there are only a very few items that have been developed to measure an objective—that is, if the test is rather short—then the level of mastery should be higher than if it is long. The main reason for this is that a short test will tend to be less reliable than a longer test, and the less reliable the test, the higher the level of mastery that should be obtained.

One question often raised in connection with discussions of mastery levels is, Should a statement about what constitutes mastery of an objective be included in the objective itself? Or stated differently, Should the minimal mastery level be stated in the objective? Generally no, for at least the following two reasons. First, the level of performance constituting mastery for one teacher might be very different from that of another. This becomes apparent when a task force of teachers in a given district attempts to generate objectives for all teachers in that district. If these district objectives include minimal mastery levels, teachers will simply modify them to fit their own particular situation. For example, students of a lower socioeconomic level attending one school in the district may perform very differently from students of a much higher socioeconomic level within the same district. A teacher in the former school may decide that mastery should be at a lower performance level than that in the latter school. A second reason for not including minimal mastery levels within every objective is that teachers would begin to feel hamstrung by the objectives. By the time the objective includes all the conditions that are necessary for its attainment, along with the minimum mastery level, it has usually been reduced from an instructional objective to a drill objective. When it reaches this degree of specification, teachers begin to feel too encumbered. Allowing individual teachers to decide what level of performance constitutes mastery is probably a more desirable procedure.

A second question concerning mastery levels is, Is there any relationship between the form of an objective and what its level of mastery can be? Yes, there is. If we have a drill objective, it becomes very difficult to develop many more than one or two different items which measure the objective. For example, suppose the drill objective is "The student will be able to correctly add two plus two." How many questions can be generated which directly measure the attainment of that objective? Just one. We present a student with a piece of paper and ask, What is two plus two? Since we have only one item, mastery or nonmastery has to be determined by the student's performance on that *one* item. If he answers the item correctly, he demonstrates complete mastery of the objective; if he misses the item, he demonstrates complete nonmastery of the objective. Thus, for very specific objectives (drill objectives), only one or two different items can be developed to measure their attainment. In such a situation, either the student answers the item correctly or incorrectly. There is no in-between score for a single item; such a situation dictates only *one* level for mastery, 100%.

As we move up from drill objectives to instructional objectives, more than one level of mastery becomes possible because we can develop *more than one* measuring item. As the objective becomes slightly more general, we are able to develop several different items which measure that objective. If there are four items measuring the same objective, for example, we could allow mastery to be either 25% and above (1/4), 50% and above (2/4), 75% and above (3/4), or 100% (4/4). We might decide that a student correctly answering three or more out of the four (75% and above) will have mastered the objective. This brings us to an important conclusion: The more different items that can be developed which measure the same objective, the more percentages available for selecting a mastery level, and, therefore, the more choices available to the teacher for deciding what should constitute mastery.

The Need for Degrees of Achievement

The foregoing discussion leads us into one of the problems of a mastery versus a nonmastery measuring orientation toward objectives. We have but two categories, either the student masters the objectives or he does not master the objectives. This is a very coarse system of evaluation. We often don't know *to what degree* a student achieved a set of objectives, only that he either achieved to a mastery level or he did not. This dilemma is well illustrated by the concerns of students who take classes on a mastery-nonmastery basis. Those students mastering the objectives are typically less concerned about the degree of their achievement. But there is considerable concern among those students who do not quite reach the mastery level. "Even though I failed to reach mastery level, I can demonstrate some degree of achievement!" What do we say to a student who achieves 70% of the objectives when 80% represents mastery? This student is relegated to the nonmastery category with some other student who has achieved, say, only 5% of the objectives. This one large category seems hardly fair. We need to be able to talk about the degree of achievement even though it may not reach a mastery level. That is, we need to make finer discriminations than simply mastery or nonmastery. We need to find out (1) whether the student has mastered

the objectives (is he above or below some cutoff level?) and (2) the degree
to which he has achieved the objectives (at what level is he?).

How Shall We Grade Instructional Objectives?

By Comparison with Other Students
or by Comparison with Some Standard?

In the last section we learned that a student's score represents the
degree to which objectives have been achieved. If a student has mastered
33% of the objectives, how do we go about assigning his grade?

A teacher's first impulse might be to ask, How does this percentage
compare with percentages of other students in the class? How does this
student's performance look relative to the rest of the class? What is his
class standing? This would be known as a *norm referenced* system of
grading. Here the teacher is not so worried about whether the student has
achieved the objective, but rather where he stands when compared
to the rest of the class. The comparison is between his performance and
that of other students. If 33% is near the top of the class, he will undoubtedly receive an *A*; if somewhat lower, perhaps a *B*, and if lower still, perhaps a *C*.

Using a norm-referenced grading system for instructional objectives
seems logical enough, especially since teachers have been grading on a
curve for years. However, teachers often find themselves in a dilemma.
Here is what happens. Suppose Mr. Carson presents his class with a clear
set of instructional objectives and voices the hope that all will attain
them. Indeed, is this not the purpose of instruction? He works diligently
with his students, providing help and learning experiences in such a way
that most of his students master the objectives. When it comes time for
grades, Mr. Carson relies upon his time-honored system of grading on a
curve. He simply places all of the students in a distribution (according to
the degree to which they have achieved the objectives) and presents the
top group with *A*'s, the middle group with *B*'s, and the bottom group with
C's. But, even the *C* students mastered the objectives! In righteous
indignation these lower-achieving students approach him and exclaim,
"If you wanted us all to attain your objectives—and we have all done
so—why the *C* grade?" Mr. Carson's only recourse is to say, "Because,
when compared to the rest of the class, you did poorly." Or in an attempt
to extricate himself from an embarrassing situation, he might reply, "You
achieved the objectives to a lesser degree than the rest of the class." Mr.
Carson wants all his students to achieve the objectives, and then punishes
them for doing so!

How can teachers prevent such unfairness in grading instructional
objectives? They can use a *criterion-referenced* grading system. Here the
student's performance is compared with some external standard or
criterion, rather than the performance of his classmates; he is graded on
whether or not he masters the objectives rather than where he stands in

relation to the rest of the class. This book has been about the establishment of these external criteria, namely, objectives. With objectives, teachers need not be concerned with a distribution of students' scores but rather with the percentage of attainment for each student. If all the students in the class master the objectives, they *all* receive *A*'s or whatever grade is equivalent to mastery! If the student is in any competition, it is against the objectives rather than against his fellow classmates. Rather than ending up with a certain percentage of *A*'s, *B*'s, and *C*'s, teachers might end up with all *A*'s or some *A*'s and *B*'s or whatever; they are not concerned with the shape of the distribution of grades.

In reporting student progress, there is often value in providing *both* norm-referenced and criterion-referenced information. Suppose parents are interested in the degree to which their child is achieving the objectives *and* his relative standing in the class. He may be mastering all of the objectives, and when compared to the rest of the class, be at the 35th percentile. A teacher might report that Johnny is mastering 50% of the objectives and is at the 70th percentile. Johnny's grade is based upon his mastery of the objectives; his percentile rank is included for the purpose of making other kinds of decisions. For example, the teacher might want to form some "ability" groupings for greater individualization of instruction; or perhaps there are to be new grade-level groupings, and the higher-achieving students are to be placed in one grade and the lower-achieving students in another; or suppose Mary starts school with mostly older children, and the teacher and parents want to see if her class ranking remains relatively constant as she moves through first, second, and third grade.

In making administrative decisions, in selecting students, and in providing for exceptional education, the availability of norm-referenced information will continue to be of great value. In grading, improving instruction, and modifying objectives, criterion-referenced information will be most helpful.

Grading Instructional Objectives:
An Example

Earlier in this area of concern we discussed the importance of deciding upon the level at which objectives are considered to be mastered. If we use the simple but coarse mastery or nonmastery classification system, only two grades are required, perhaps pass-fail or *A-C* or whatever each teacher decides upon. We also mentioned the unfairness of grouping students with large differences in achievement into the same category. (This practice is not unlike traditional beliefs in Heaven and Hell. If Mr. Brown does one more good deed than Mrs. Brown, he goes clear to Heaven and she winds up in Hell.) Because a simple pass-fail system has no further gradations, it may be less fair to students than they realize. What we need are more categories while still maintaining a criterion-referenced grading system. The author has experimented with several varieties of grading systems for instructional objectives, none of which have been optimally satisfying. Following is an example of how a grading system for instructional objectives might work.

Suppose there are nine general topics to be covered during a course. Suppose also there are objectives generated for each topic. For topic 1 there are five objectives, for topic 2 there are fifteen, and so on. Suppose there are 115 objectives generated from these nine topics and five test items for each of the 115 objectives, making a total of 575 items. Since there is only one grade for the entire course and since it is determined at the end of the course, an arbitrary decision is made as to what percentage of these 575 items needs to be correctly answered for mastery of the objectives taken as a group. (Attempting to keep track of mastery or nonmastery for each separate objective for every student would turn out to be a herculean task!) Suppose mastery of the objectives constitutes correctly answering 50% of all the items, or a score of 288. (Since this mastery level was established of the basis of performance of past classes, we are still left with the realization that a criterion-referenced evaluation has emerged from norm-referenced data.) Obviously, the student would not be expected to take all 575 items in one sitting; as such, there might be three different evaluations, each evaluation covering the objectives under, say, just three topics. The student does not master or nonmaster the objectives in each exam, but rather the total group of objectives at the end of the course. Theoretically, a student should be examined on these objectives until he finally masters them; in reality, time and energy limitations prevent more than about two attempts. If the student fails to master the objectives in two attempts, he is simply given an "Incomplete" until he is able to reach that level after more instruction.

As mentioned earlier, a mastery-nonmastery grading system is too coarse. Some students will consistently achieve just less than 50% of the objectives, and it seems unfair to give them a nonmastery grade along with students achieving only 10% of the objectives. In an attempt to achieve greater fairness, the teacher might think in terms of degree of achievement. The reasoning goes as follows. A student correctly answering 60% of the items is considered to have achieved fewer objectives than a student correctly answering 70%, and he in turn, less than a person correctly answering 80%. In order to master the objectives, a student must correctly answer 50% of the items. Here he has no choice. This has been arbitrarily designated as the minimal level at which the student must function if he is to be successful in the course. If he achieves 50% or above (mastery) he might be given at least a C. Above the mastery level, he now has some choices. If he wants a B, he must achieve 70% of the objectives (correctly answer 70% of the items); if he wants an A, 80% of the objectives must be achieved. Thus this system provides not only a mastery-nonmastery classification (above or below 50%), but also the degree of achievement (0% to 100%).

Figure 3.   Sample Grade Slip (Appropriate for High School and College)

Name: Bert Lang
Class: History 131

1. Percentage of objectives achieved: 83%

2. Objectives were MASTERED — NONMASTERED.

3. Percentile rank of student: 72

In summary, the grading of instructional objectives might occur in at least two ways. A simple procedure is to give grades of pass-fail or mastery-nonmastery. To be fair to the students and also to provide more information about each student, more gradations are desirable. We can achieve this by determining the degree of achievement in addition to mastery or nonmastery.

Making Up Report Cards
Based upon Instructional Objectives
Let us take a brief look at some possible formats for report cards that would be compatible with the use of instructional objectives. Generally, the traditional letter grading system *(A, B, C, D)* of reporting pupil progress does not lend itself very well to instructional objectives. Letter grades have been so closely linked with the student's relative standing in a group that they are not readily applied to a situation where a student is compared to some criterion.

One possible format would be simply a slip of paper containing three bits of information, without any listing of the instructional objectives (see Figure 3). This format might be used in situations where there are large numbers of objectives and the pupil progress is reported only once, at the end of the course. Some high school classes and college courses might lend themselves to this type of reporting. The slip would contain (1) the percentage of objectives achieved, (2) a statement as to whether this percentage reached mastery level, and (3) the student's relative standing in the class. If there must be a letter grade placed on the report card for administrative purposes or because the school requires grades, this grade should be based upon (1) and (2) but not (3).

Another possible format, more detailed and informative in nature, could be used for younger learners, perhaps kindergarten through grade 6. This would have a "continuous progress" feature and could be used throughout the year. Since a single sheet cannot possibly accommodate all of the teacher's specific instructional objectives, only more general objectives should be listed on the form itself. However, attached to this sheet might be a packet containing all of the teacher's instructional objectives should the parent be interested.

A simplified version of the above would be to list the general

Figure 4. Sample Report Card (Appropriate for Grades K–6)

Name: Susan Brown
Class: Reading
Grade: 2

General Objective	Instructional Objectives	Mastery	Nonmastery	Percentile Rank of Student
The student will be able to demonstrate:				
1. Inferential comprehension	17	X		33
2. Literal comprehension	12		X	25
3. Vocabulary comprehension	15	X		30
4. Creative activity	16	X		31
5. Study skills	12	X		31
		4	1	Average = 30

Percent Mastered = 80%

objectives, along with the number of instructional objectives included in each (see Figure 4). There would be places to indicate mastery or nonmastery for each general objective along with the student's relative standing in the class. The teacher would place a mark opposite each objective, either stopping at this point or tallying up the marks in each column for comparison purposes or for determining the percent mastered. Thus the teacher might end up with four objectives mastered and one nonmastered, for 80%. Finally, the student's average class standing on the objectives could be noted.

A slightly more involved version appears in Figure 5 which provides some additional information, the percent achievement for each general objective. Note that general objective 1 includes seventeen instructional objectives. Suppose there are three items for each of the seventeen objectives, making a total of fifty-one items. Suppose also the student correctly answers forty of these fifty-one for a percent achievement of 78%. And so it goes through the other four objectives.

Suppose mastery for each of the five *general* objectives is 60%. In Figure 5, only objective 2 is nonmastered with a percent achievement of 50%. The average percent achievement for all five general objectives is 64%. In addition, the student's relative standing (percentile rank) in the class is listed for each objective, as well as his average relative standing. It is interesting to note that even though the student easily masters all but one objective, he is only at the 30th percentile when compared to the rest of the class. Here also, grades should be based upon percent achievement rather than relative standing.

Figure 5. Sample Report Card (Appropriate For Grades K-6)

Name: Susan Brown
Class: Reading
Grade: 2

General Objective	Instructional Objectives	Percent Achievement	Mastery	Nonmastery	Percentile Rank of Student
The student will be able to demonstrate:					
1. Inferential comprehension	17	78%	X		33
2. Literal comprehension	12	50%		X	25
3. Vocabulary comprehension	15	68%	X		30
4. Creative activity	16	73%	X		31
5. Study skills	12	70%	X		31
		Mean Percent Achievement = 64%			Mean Percentile Rank = 30

These are but several of any number of reporting formats teachers might consider. In each case, the student objectives are listed, not what the teacher has covered over the course of the year.

Suggestions for the Teacher Emerging
from This Area of Concern

1. In general, you should try to base more of your evaluation on systematic and rigorously conducted measurement.
2. All your measuring instruments should have adequate content validity; that is, the measuring instrument should call forth behaviors and topics that are as similar as possible to those identified in the objectives.
3. All your measuring instruments should have adequate reliability; that is, they should be consistent in measuring whatever they measure. This consistency can be improved by increasing the number of items in the measuring instrument.
4. You should not allow available measuring instruments to dictate what types of objectives you generate; rather, the objectives should dictate the types of measuring instruments to be selected or developed.
5. When using instructional objectives, you should be more concerned with the validity of a measuring instrument than with its reliability.
6. You should develop at least three (and whenever possible, more) different items for each objective to be measured.
7. You should vary in difficulty the items developed for an objective, ranging them from easy to difficult.
8. Your measuring items should be answered correctly by more students after instruction than before instruction.
9. In measuring objectives, you should generally be more concerned about comparing the student's performance with some "ideal" performance than simply with his growth over a period of time.
10. You need to know more than simply whether an objective is "mastered" or "nonmastered"; in addition, you should know the *degree* to which an objective is achieved. Does this degree of achievement reach a "mastery" level?
11. Generally, the minimal level of acceptable performance should *not* be included in an objective. You should be free to set your own level.
12. When using instructional objectives in class, you should not grade on a curve. Your grades should be based upon the percentage of objectives mastered rather than a student's relative standing in the class.

Area of Concern Thirteen:
What Effects Do Instructional Objectives Have on Individual Differences?

Over the past several years, there has been an increasing concern for and commitment to a greater individualization of instruction. Giving rise to this trend has been the realization by most teachers that individual differences need to be more effectively accommodated during instructional experiences. Likewise there is an increasing belief among teachers that students should amplify or at least maintain their differences, rather than minimize them. There is an acute awareness that these differences, when gathered together in traditional classrooms, begin to disappear as a result of classroom instruction. Thus we now see a pronounced trend toward greater individualization to heighten the uniqueness among students and to capitalize on individual learning styles. While in practice this particular commitment is not yet pervasive, the concern among teachers is widespread.

A frequent criticism leveled by teachers when exposed to instructional objectives is, "If I am asked to develop instructional objectives for my students, and if these objectives are attained by all of my students, then they will all be performing the same behaviors toward the same content. They will all look alike, not different! If this is the case, then instructional objectives will serve to minimize and reduce individual differences when in fact I really want to increase them!"

Let us think through this charge. First of all, we need to be careful to sort out those areas in which we definitely want students to differ from those in which we want them all to be the same. Surprisingly, there are a great many behaviors and topics in the existing curriculum in which teachers do *not* want students to differ. Examples are sharpening a pencil, adding two columns of numbers, finding a square root, spelling words, pronouncing words, typing, knowing techniques used in hemstitching a dress, displaying proper pole-vaulting techniques, identifying state capitals in the United States, using rules of grammar, and a great many more.

A second look at this charge leaves us with some confusion about what teachers mean when talking about "individual differences" and "individualized instruction." There are several possibilities. We can think about differences among students such as motivation, learning style, preference for mode of learning, speed of learning, rate of forgetting, and so on. Or we might think about differences in the instruction itself, such as having different objectives for each student, having the same objectives but different learning experiences, or a combination of both. There are several ways we can think about individualizing instruction for individual differences, and teachers need to be specific about what they mean in each case.

Having instructional objectives per se appears to have no effect whatsoever on increasing or decreasing individual differences. The *way* an objective is stated, however, does produce very marked effects. An objective can be stated so as to increase individual differences or to decrease them; for example, "The student will be able to recite the multiplication tables for one through ten." This objective will have all the students doing the same thing, reciting combinations of numbers from one through ten. Here we minimize both differences in behaviors and topics studied by the students. Indeed, here is a case where they all perform exactly the same behaviors and study exactly the same topics. Now suppose another objective: "Each student will develop a project which differs in some way from every other project in the class." Here is an objective which maximizes individual differences in both behaviors and topics studied. Following are further examples:

1. The student will be able to explain the workings of an internal combustion engine after having studied it through any source he chooses. (Here, all students have the same objective, but differences occur in the instruction.)
2. The student will select his own topic, study it through sources which are most helpful to him, and describe verbally or in writing how the topic can be used in his own life. (Here, again, each student has the same objective—describing how the topic can be applied in his life—but differences occur in the means to achieve that objective—through each student's own sources.)
3. Given a list of objectives, the student will select the one which is of greatest interest to him and achieve it through any resources available in the room. (Here differences occur in both the objectives and the instructional experiences.)
4. For the unit on Brazil, the student will be able to define his own objectives and reach them through sources available in the classroom. (Here, again, differences occur in both the objectives and the instruction.)

We observe, then, that the way an objective is stated determines whether it will increase or decrease various kinds of differences among students. Up until now, teachers have generated objectives which mostly bring about a decrease in individual differences. Since their commitments are usually in the opposite direction, a logical conclusion is that they have just not had enough experience in generating objectives which increase differences. Instructional objectives can be a powerful method for either increasing or decreasing individual differences and, if teachers are committed to greater individualization of instruction, they can effectively use instructional objectives to amplify almost any differences among students.

What Happens When a Teacher Suddenly Switches to the Use of Instructional Objectives?

Suppose we have a typical senior high school classroom with thirty students and one teacher. This teacher has twelve years of teaching experience and suddenly decides to start using specific instructional objectives in teaching. What changes occur among the students that might either cause problems or develop into more desirable consequences? (These probable changes are based on the assumption that the objectives are clearly stated, the students understand them, and do in fact use them.)

There will be a tendency for some already-existing differences to increase and decrease. Because the student is now less controlled by the teacher's lectures and discussions in class, the faster students move out and go even faster, while the slower students, who have been rushed along in order to keep up, slow down to a more leisurely pace. Thus, the differences among students in the *speed* with which they learn new material actually increase. On the other hand, differences among students in the *degree* to which they learn material decrease. This is because the slower students can now stay with the material until they have mastered it to about the same degree as the faster students; before, the pace kept them continually on the run, and they lacked the time for more thorough learning. Finally, a greater percentage of the students now learn the material. In sum, students become increasingly different in the speed with which they learn material; at the same time, they become increasingly similar in the extent to which they learn the material.

The author has observed these differences at the college level during several years of teaching with instructional objectives. Some students complete the course objectives in six to ten weeks, while others require as much as twenty-four weeks. Granted some of this increased variation is due to the removal of deadlines; much of it, however, is due to the "preferred rate of learning" of each student. Secondly, when provided with freedom for self-pacing, students seem to exhibit less variation in the degree to which they obtain the objectives. That is, the standard deviations on the tests become smaller.

How Can a Teacher Individualize Instruction
to a Greater Degree
Through the Use of Instructional Objectives?

One of the more obvious approaches for individualizing instruction would be to have different objectives for each student. A third-grade teacher with a class of thirty students might develop a completely different set of objectives for each pupil. While such a procedure is most honorable, in practice it turns out to be extremely ambitious. Maintaining a separate set of objectives for each student in the class becomes virtually unmanageable. Each student needs his own set of instructional materials, along with his own separate teacher, not to mention his own evaluation and management systems.

A teacher can, however, begin to approximate such an ideal. One possibility is to generate a set of "core" objectives for the entire class and then have some "optional" objectives for certain students who quickly and easily master the core objectives or who have unusual difficulty with them. Another possibility is to have one set of objectives for the slower-achieving students, one set for the middle-achieving students, and one set for the high-achieving students. This latter plan has not been implemented as effectively as the former. Another possibility would be to have some units for which students can design their own objectives and other units for which the teacher takes total responsibility. This procedure allows the students to participate, to some extent, in the selection of their own instructional objectives. Finally, another possibility would be to generate—from the same general educational objective—instructional objectives tailored to each age level. For example, suppose the following educational objective: "The student will be able to relate more effectively to those around him." From this objective, a teacher at the kindergarten level would undoubtedly generate a different set of instructional objectives than would a teacher at the first-grade level and one from the second-grade level. They all use the same general objective but different, localized instructional objectives.

A second method for individualizing instruction is to have the same objectives for all students but vary the means for attaining them. In the foregoing procedure, the teacher provided differences among ends; here we are talking about differences among means for a common end. Suppose our third-grade class is given this common objective: "Each student will be able to sing a simple song on pitch and follow the correct beat." We may even want all the students to sing the same song, but notice the variability that could be provided in the methods used to learn the song. Some students may choose to have the song sung for them time after time until they can imitate the demonstrator; other students may prefer to listen to a record replayed many times; still other students may prefer to take the song home and have their mothers teach it to them on their own piano. Thus there are a variety of methods a child might use to achieve this simple objective. Though individualizing the means is probably easier than individualizing the ends, there are still limitations such as available money to purchase a variety of instructional materials, more instructional space, teacher time, and overall management.

It might be worthwhile to note at this point that some schools are moving toward an individually prescribed instruction in which students work through Learning Activity Packages (LAPS). Each student receives a package which includes a set of objectives, a variety of instructional sources to which he might go, and an evaluation. Even with this system of receiving a combination of written, spoken, and visual sources, considerable teacher attention and management must be provided. Nonetheless, in spite of such limitations, a teacher in virtually any classroom setting can, to a large degree, individualize instructional experiences, and to a lesser degree, student objectives.

Through the use of instructional objectives, there are other activities teachers might perform to make instruction more individualized. Not to be underestimated is the freedom single teachers enjoy in generating their own personal set of' objectives for their own classes. This source provides individualization among teachers rather than among students. Also, teachers might designate different mastery levels for different students in their classes. Some students may be expected to achieve at one level for mastery; other students, at a different level. (In making up some type of instructional packet at a district-wide level, one might include (1) instructional objectives without specifying a level of acceptable performance, (2) sources and suggested materials *for teachers* so they can make up their own particular lesson plans, and (3) actual evaluations for the objectives.)

Additionally, teachers can continue to provide more individual pacing in their classrooms. By allowing each student to take as much or as little time as is necessary to attain the objectives, teachers begin to contribute to individual styles of learning. In contrast to this individual pacing, many students in our schools today are products of an extremely rigid pacing system. They have become habituated to move only when external motivation is imposed; thus, they encounter initial difficulty when such freedom is granted to them. However, the introduction of at least some self-pacing at early ages should produce more independent tendencies at later age levels.

Suggestions for the Teacher Emerging
from This Area of Concern

1. You should be careful to be precise in identifying what you mean when talking about "individualized instruction."
2. Since instructional objectives are an effective means for increasing *or*

decreasing differences among students, if you are interested in more individualization, you can profit by their use.

3. You should experiment more with individualized objectives. One possible way to achieve differences in objectives is to generate a set of "core" objectives and a set of "optional" objectives for the various types of learners in the class.

4. Individualization can occur in both instructional experiences and instructional outcomes. For the present, you will no doubt find it easier to individualize your instruction than to individualize your objectives. That is, it may be easier to have common objectives for all students, with a variety of means for attaining them, than to have different objectives for each student.

Area of Concern Fourteen:
Who Should Be Responsible
for Developing Objectives,
and What Sources Are Available?

If teachers are becoming more accountable for their actions within the classroom, then it seems consistent to expect other people who are concerned with public education to likewise feel increasingly accountable. The questions of who should be responsible for bringing about changes within the student and what these changes should be are taking on increasing importance.

The discussion in this area of concern is based upon the belief that an ever-widening circle of people should take on responsibility for the development of objectives. At first thought, it seems natural for teachers to be charged with complete responsibility for developing objectives for their students. Even though this is what most frequently happens, we need to begin bringing in more and more people to share in this decision-making process. This is not to suggest that all elements of the society should be involved with the development of specific instructional objectives in the classroom; but it does mean that all elements should be represented in suggesting educational objectives.

People Who Either Directly or Indirectly
Influence Instructional Objectives

People in the Educational Community
The students themselves are the very heart of the educational process. They influence which objectives the teacher will choose for them. Sometimes they are invited to participate, and other times they do so on their own, either on purpose or unintentionally. For example, much of the student unrest on campuses across the nation can be traced to irrelevant objectives; this pressure has caused many professors to soul-search about the instructional objectives they use.

Teachers are no doubt more responsible for instructional objectives than any other persons. Either intentionally or without knowing, they are mostly responsible for what learning occurs in their classrooms.

Moving outside the immediate classrooms, school principals exercise considerable influence on the instructional objectives to be taught since their overall school policies find voice in both the teachers' objectives and their methods of reaching them. Suppose, for example, an objective a principal might have for an entire staff: "Teachers will be able to develop greater independence in their students." As this is continually emphasized in faculty and curriculum planning sessions, teachers begin to notice their instructional objectives include such things as: "The student will be able to select his own materials for making projects of his choice."

There are many people at the district level who indirectly influence teachers' instructional objectives. Teacher committees formed by the district are brought together for the purpose of generating district objectives that can be used in the classroom; curriculum specialists, directors of curriculum, and assistant superintendents are often found on these committees and provide their own input from the district's point of view. Also, members of neighboring school districts visit for the purpose of information gathering and, while present, leave many of their own ideas about objectives. University people coming in as curriculum or evaluation consultants likewise influence teachers' instructional objectives. Finally, state offices of education, through funding, hiring practices, policies, and visiting personnel provide considerable influence on objectives found in the classroom.

People in the Noneducational Community

More people not directly involved in education are influencing teachers as they work on objectives. Sometimes this influence is subtle and other times direct. Parents exert considerable impact through P.T.A., individual conferences with a teacher, responses to surveys sent out by the school, and through their own children.

Local and federal governments act in peculiar ways to influence the teacher's objectives. Some of these turn out to be direct and powerful. For example, funds from the federal government for certain types of programs affect teachers in the classroom. Suppose a program for inquiry training is funded for development by a specific regional laboratory. People from the laboratory approach teachers in the area with special training programs on how to develop inquiry skills. Once the teachers are trained, they notice themselves developing inquiry-skill objectives for their students like the following: "The student will have developed appropriate inquiry skills in science."

There are some indirect, but as it turns out, rather effective ways that federal funding to a local school district can influence the type of objectives teachers will develop for their classes. Suppose, for example, a school district is funded for the development of various kinds of "open-concept" educational programs. Coupled with state funds, some of this federal money goes into the construction of an open-concept facility. One of the first tasks of the new staff moving into the building is to decide what kinds of objectives will be best achieved through this particular school structure. Understandably, teachers begin to generate "open-concept" objectives such as "The student will use a wider variety of sources and teachers in studying a unit"; "The student will feel greater freedom and independence in his study program"; "The student will be able to move from one task to another by himself"; and so on.

Another agency entering the educational scene with alarming influence is private industry. The time approaches when education will be private industry's major customer. Many firms are successfully selling packaged instruction and management systems to school districts throughout the country. While private industry's potential contribution to education cannot be overstated—especially in the area of technology and hardware—educators must beware of underdeveloped and unrefined programs that have not as yet undergone serious evaluation. Whenever a school district purchases a program of learning packages from a firm, it is also, in effect, buying some instructional objectives. There is nothing wrong with this if the objectives in the program are considered appropriate by educators in that school district. If the program's objectives are incomplete and cannot be integrated with the district's overall set of objectives, serious difficulties arise. Once a company has contracted with the school district and "moved in," a dangerous entrenchment is only a small step away. The program will go on for three or four years based solely on its original momentum and the district's heavy financial commitment. Evaluations are frequently superficial or quietly forgotten, and teachers within the district become strapped with a set of unwanted instructional objectives simply because they agreed to "try out" the new program. The future impact of private industry upon specific instructional objectives may be far more powerful than we now realize.

Finally, an agency combining members of the educational and noneducational community is the school board. The deliberations, concerns, and interactions of school board members with school personnel will always continue to have a direct impact upon teacher's objectives in the classroom.

Who Should Be Responsible
for Developing Objectives?

If objectives become a more permanent and formalized part of current and future instruction, what people should be responsible for their development? All people in both the educational and noneducational communities should work on these objectives at some level. The educational and noneducational communities outside the immediate classroom should probably lend their attention to generating the more broad educational objectives. Those people closer to the actual classroom (e.g., the district curriculum committee and teacher committees working on instruction) should spend most of their efforts in translating general educational objectives into general instructional objectives. Finally, the teacher in the classroom, and, when appropriate, the student have the major responsibility for generating specific instructional objectives that will be taught. Thus people further away from the classroom itself should have more responsibility for the educational objectives, whereas those closest to the classroom should be most responsible for instructional objectives.

It is important that we begin to build a closer relationship between educational and instructional objectives. One way to do this is to provide training for people in the educational and noneducational communities outside the classroom in how to develop legitimate educational objectives; this will facilitate the translation of educational objectives into instructional objectives by other people nearer the actual classroom, because instructional objectives are more easily generated from general objectives than from statements of philosophy or values.

Certainly one of the key tasks in the near future will be that of taking broad educational objectives and using them as guidelines for the generation of more specific instructional objectives. Therefore, some sort of working relationship in this specific area needs to be established among teachers, curriculum specialists at the district level, and anyone else confronted with the responsibility of developing general educational objectives. It is crucial that the teacher be sensitive to educational objectives developed by people outside the classroom and that they, in turn, be sensitive to instructional objectives developed by the teacher. This division of labor will also help develop a division of expertise. People with varied backgrounds in the community will become more skillful in developing educational objectives, while teachers will improve their skill of generating instructional objectives.

What Sources Are Available for Obtaining Educational and Instructional Objectives?

The majority of published manuals on how to write behavioral objectives contain a section on sources in which can be found examples of behavioral objectives. (The extensive bibliography at the end of this book contains sources *about* instructional objectives, not examples of them.) Most of the teachers who go to sources that do give examples come away less than satisfied. There are several reasons for this. First, these sources generally turn out to be something other than legitimate objectives. They are usually in the form of behaviors (e.g., the Bloom-Group Taxonomies) or in the form of subject matter (e.g., scope and sequences). Second, when legitimate objectives are located, they are usually educational rather than instructional objectives, and they are often outdated. Third, the objectives can seldom be adopted into a teacher's curriculum because so many will appear inappropriate in terms of the teacher's own objectives.

If teachers are interested in some examples of *instructional* objectives either to examine, select from, or adopt, two sources have proven helpful. First, securing instructional objectives developed by other schools or other districts either close by or across the nation is useful. Schools and school districts in many sections of the country are developing impressively complete and functional instructional objectives; indeed, the rate at which this is occurring suggests the importance of developing better communications among districts. After struggling for five months to generate district-wide math objectives, a given school district is embarrassed to learn that a neighboring district went through the process a year earlier, emerging with a strikingly similar set of math objectives! And a telephone call would have saved about four months' work! Objectives from this source are up-to-date, often well organized, and frequently well conceived.

A second source which is increasingly used is the objectives "bank" located in the Instructional Objectives Exchange, originally affiliated with the Center for the Study of Evaluation at U.C.L.A. in Los Angeles. Teachers have used objectives from this source with varying degrees of satisfaction. Literature teachers reading through the catalogued objectives in literature would probably select some objectives, modify others, and use still others to trigger off the development of their own objectives. Teachers have also experienced some frustrations, however, in attempting to use objectives from this source. Some of them are poorly constructed and some of the evaluation items are invalid; sometimes, if the objectives are used in one subject-matter field and not another, the overall curriculum becomes unbalanced. Finally, selecting already-developed objectives often takes longer than generating them from scratch. However, this "bank" represents an ambitious and commendable start at the nation-wide level.

There are other sources which teachers consistently use, but these are not sources of complete objectives; they are sources of various parts of objectives, most typically the topic or subject-matter part. Teachers go to various subject-matter sources and then generate their own objectives. Interestingly, subject-matter guides represent the most frequent source used by teachers. Some of the more common subject-matter or topic sources are: teacher editions of a textbook, student texts, curriculum subject-matter guides, current lesson plans, books on various subjects found in the district curriculum library, and the teacher's own personal experience (college training, years in the classroom, discussions with other teachers in the field, etc.).

A variety of sources does not necessarily facilitate the task of generating instructional objectives; it does, however, provide teachers with valuable checklists. A math teacher, for example, does have some responsibility to look around and see what other math teachers feel is important to teach and what is not so important. A variety of sources will allow teachers to see if some important objectives are being excluded, or if they need to change areas of emphasis. For this reason, teachers should gather as many different sources as possible, mainly to verify their own objectives.

Suggestions for the Teacher Emerging from This Area of Concern

1. Before sitting down to generate instructional objectives, you should try to obtain any relevant educational objectives already developed by members of the educational and noneducational community
2. For the present, the most fruitful sources for finding instructional objectives are (1) schools and school districts that have already generated instructional objectives for their programs, (2) the Instructional Objectives Exchange, and (3) other teachers who have past experience in teaching the subject matter and, therefore, a variety of subject-matter sources available to them.

Area of Concern Fifteen:
How Usable Is a Taxonomy
of Educational Objectives?

What Is a Taxonomy of Educational Objectives,
and What Is It Supposed to Do?

A *taxonomy* is simply a scheme for classifying certain things in a particular order. Thus, a taxonomy of educational objectives is a scheme for classifying educational objectives in some particular order. Over a period of time, between 1949 and 1956, certain people attending conferences discussed the possibility of developing some sort of taxonomy of educational objectives. These discussions ultimately led to the formal publication of *Taxonomy of Educational Objectives: Cognitive Domain.* This book appeared in 1956, with Benjamin S. Bloom as the editor and Max Engelhart, Edward Furst, Walker Hill, and David Krathwohl as committee members. Several years later, in 1964, another volume entitled *Taxonomy of Educational Objectives: Affective Domain* was written by some of the members of the original committee, namely David Krathwohl and Benjamin Bloom, with a new member, Bertram Masia. In our discussion, these two volumes will be referred to as the Bloom-Group Taxonomies. These two groups of people embarked on a rather ambitious and historic undertaking, namely, that of building taxonomies of educational objectives in the *cognitive* and *affective* domains. These taxonomies will be only briefly described here. For further study, you are directed to the taxonomies themselves.

Let us look at the taxonomy of the cognitive domain. After considerable work, the group determined six major cognitive behaviors they felt pervaded most of the objectives teachers generated in the public education system. These six behaviors were placed in a hierarchy from simple to complex; then each of the major behaviors was broken down into more specific behaviors. The six behaviors, from most simple to most complex, are *knowledge, comprehension, application, analysis, synthesis,* and *evaluation.* Following are examples of how some of the behaviors were further broken down. In the *knowledge* category, we find knowledge of specifics, knowledge of ways and means of dealing with specifics, and knowledge of the universals and abstractions in a field. Here again, the ranking is from simple to complex within the major category. If we examine the second major category, *comprehension,* we see that the more specific behaviors are translation, interpretation, and extrapolation. This same pattern exists throughout all of the categories. In addition to this classification scheme, test questions, designed to measure each of these major behaviors and their more specific subdivisions, are included.

Essentially the same general pattern as above was followed in the taxonomy for the affective domain. For this domain, the group emerged with five major affective behaviors. These are also placed in a hierarchical arrangement from behaviors that have low internalization to behaviors that have rather high internalization. From low to high, they are as follows: *receiving* or *attending, responding, valuing, organization,* and *characterization by a value or a value complex.* Here again, each major behavior is broken down into subdivisions. For example, the behavior *receiving* is broken down into awareness, willingness to receive, and controlled or selected attention. These affective behaviors may be less familiar to teachers, but they roughly parallel the more familiar terms used by teachers: interest, appreciation, attitude, value, adjustment.

We need not become more familiar with these taxonomies to observe that the cognitive domain represents intellectual or "thinking" behaviors, while the affective domain refers to feelings, attitudes, interests, and values. A taxonomy of objectives in a third domain, the *psychomotor* (manipulative or motor skill), is currently being compiled.

The purported uses of this taxonomy of educational objectives are:

1. A taxonomy helps people communicate by forcing them to use more precise language.
2. A taxonomy provides teachers with a wide range of possible educational outcomes from which to select.
3. A taxonomy provides teachers, if they place all their objectives within the taxonomy, with a picture of those objectives that have been given considerable emphasis and those that have been generally omitted. Some of the categories will be very full and others will be relatively empty.
4. A taxonomy helps teachers specify objectives so learning experiences can be more easily planned.
5. A taxonomy helps teachers evaluate objectives and modify them.
6. A taxonomy helps teachers determine the appropriateness of the instruction and evaluation being used.
7. A taxonomy facilitates research in the area of objectives and instruction.

Why Have Teachers—in Actual Practice—
Encountered Difficulty in Using the Bloom-Group Taxonomies?

In workshop after workshop, the author has repeatedly observed frustration among teachers as they have attempted to use the Bloom-

Group Taxonomies in generating their own instructional objectives. These taxonomies have been less helpful to teachers for what appear to be the following reasons.

1. The taxonomies are statements of behaviors only. Teachers have difficulty attempting to fit complete objectives (behaviors and topics) into a taxonomy of behaviors. That is, the behavior alone does not constitute a complete objective. Thus these may be more accurately called taxonomies of educational behaviors.

2. A taxonomy of behaviors provides little help in taxonomizing topics or subject matter. Teachers have consistently felt the need to classify subject matter into categories such as facts, concepts, principles, generalizations, etc. Taxonomies of behaviors offer little assistance here.

3. There are many important behaviors not included in the taxonomies. For example, in the cognitive domain, behaviors like *add, write, pronounce, spell, read,* and *compute* are not included. Though many teachers have tried to include these behaviors under "application," they have found that they are far too complex to lend themselves totally to such a categorization. Thus, teachers have had considerable difficulty in attempting to decide where to place behaviors such as those above.

4. The cognitive domain leaves much to be desired for those curriculum areas which are not strictly subject-matter areas. That is, while areas like history and biology lend themselves easily to the use of cognitive behaviors specified in the taxonomy, other fields like typing, music, art, and dramatics do not. For example, cognitive behaviors in learning to type probably do not involve much comprehension, application, analysis, synthesis, and evaluation. Also, how much application, analysis, synthesis, and evaluation are used in the cognitive behaviors involved in art or dramatics?

5. The taxonomy for the cognitive domain has been easier to use than the taxonomy for the affective domain. The former is more complete, detailed, and carefully worked out. But since 1956, there has been a distinct trend to place more emphasis on affective objectives. Thus, teachers in the seventies who may be more committed to affective objectives than teachers in the fifties are presented with a less detailed and less understandable taxonomy from which to select their affective objectives.

6. Teachers are frequently overwhelmed by the taxonomies. There are so many behaviors, teachers become prematurely discouraged.

7. If teachers from all areas of the curriculum are brought together and presented with, say, the taxonomy of the cognitive domain, it becomes quickly apparent that its six major behaviors do not pervade an entire curriculum. To be sure, the behaviors are widespread in *subject-matter* areas. But, what about teachers who want to generate objectives in areas like woodcarving, sheet-metal work, physical education, cooking, sewing, and counseling? These areas cannot be assigned to the affective

or psychomotor domains, because they do have cognitive behaviors, but apparently not the exact kind found in the cognitive domain. Stated somewhat differently, there are areas which have their own unique behaviors, which are not in any sense pervasive throughout the entire curriculum. For example, in math there are unique behaviors like computing, adding, subtracting, factoring, etc. How do teachers relate these to knowing, comprehending, applying, etc.? Here are some other examples: Spelling, pronouncing, and writing are unique to the area of language arts; transcribing notes from one key to another key is unique to music; balancing an equation is unique to mathematics. Thus there are many cognitive behaviors unique to a particular area that are not identified in the taxonomies.

8. Too many teachers accept these taxonomies as gospel truth. A teacher might be heard to say "Unless I have the student knowing, comprehending, applying, analyzing, synthesizing, and evaluating this particular subject matter, he won't really have learned it"; or "How can I teach him to conceptualize until he has memorized?"

9. The taxonomy of the cognitive domain has limited use for young children. Primary teachers consider it a little unrealistic to develop application, analysis, synthesis, and evaluation objectives for kindergarten or first-grade children.

The foregoing list represents difficulties teachers seem to encounter as they attempt to use the Bloom-Group Taxonomies in generating their own instructional objectives. Following are some additional concerns that might be raised about the taxonomies themselves.

1. Attempting to divide a group of teacher-developed objectives into various "domains" (e.g., cognitive or affective) serves little if any useful purpose. First of all, these are simply arbitrarily established categories. Second, there is no confirming way to decide whether teachers have accurately placed an objective in one or the other domains. Third, these domains are not independent of each other. Thus, teachers are typically unable to find *any* behavior that can be placed exclusively in one domain.

2. The assumption of a hierarchy of learning is still open to question. There is very little direct research which suggests that simpler behaviors must be acquired before more complex behaviors can be acquired—that is, that knowledge must occur before comprehension, which in turn must occur before application, which must occur before analysis, and so on. The authors of the taxonomy do suggest that students have more difficulty answering questions measuring the higher-level behaviors than they do answering questions measuring the lower-level behaviors. However, just because one behavior is more difficult to acquire than another behavior does not mean that difficult behaviors must be learned only after simple behaviors.

3. All six of the general behaviors in the cognitive domain are mostly

covert in form. That is, knowing, comprehending, applying, analyzing, synthesizing, and evaluating are all generally unobservable behaviors. The only method presented for transforming these covert behaviors into overt behaviors is through test questions. But test items are supposed to only sample the objectives. If there are no overt behavioral objectives, then we are left with no alternative but to say that the few test items *are* the objectives.

4. Since the various levels within the cognitive domain are arbitrarily established, arguing that we should be teaching for "higher levels" is a less than meaningful activity. That is, we now hear teachers asking for more analysis, evaluation, and synthesis behaviors but for less knowledge behavior. Yet we have little solid evidence that analyzing and synthesizing are somehow on a "higher level" than memorizing.

5. A behavior placed in one context can have a considerably different meaning when it is placed in another context; not only that, the same behavior in different contexts would appropriately fit at several different levels in the hierarchy. Therefore the ranking of behaviors without a context is not a meaningful activity. Let us consider an example. Suppose we have the behavior "state." Here is one objective: "The student will be able to *state* the names of the past three presidents of the United States." This objective would probably fall at the knowledge level of the cognitive domain. But try another objective: "After applying Parkinson's law to family finance planning, the student will be able to *state* his conclusions." This objective would fit most appropriately at the application level. Now consider still a third objective: "The student will be able to *state* his analysis of the 1968 presidential campaign results." This particular objective would fit most appropriately at the analysis level of the cognitive domain. Here then, we see how the behavior "state" can fit at three different levels within the domain, with the context in which the behavior is used determining that level.

There would be fewer problems in using the taxonomy if all the behaviors in it were placed in specific contexts. However, since they are presented without contexts (standing alone), teachers become confused. For example, the behavior "translate" would, according to the taxonomy, fall at level 2 under "comprehension." Suppose a teacher constructs an objective using the behavior "translate," but in such a way that the objective appropriately falls at level 5, "synthesis." Now the teacher is in a dilemma. The entire objective is more like a "synthesis" objective, but the behavior being used, standing by itself, is supposed to fit into the second category, "comprehension."

6. The taxonomy assumes that the learner can and does acquire a behavior apart from any particular context and that this behavior can stand as an objective in and of itself. For example, the taxonomy implies that the following can be a legitimate objective: "The student will be able to analyze." The question arises whether a learner can become an analyzer apart from anything to analyze. That is, can a learner become

an analyzer in general, analyzing any specific thing that comes along? Perhaps we make this assumption, but in our actual teaching, we teach the student to analyze particular kinds of things. We give him *contexts* in which to analyze. For example, we may want the student to be able to analyze unknowns in chemistry, or we may want him to analyze problems of city government, or we may want him to analyze philosophical problems, or social problems, or adjustment problems, or whatever. But we never ask him to just plain analyze! We can legitimately generalize from analyzing in one specific context to analyzing in another specific context, but it is not fair to generalize from analyzing in specific contexts to analyzing in general. This, in effect, is what the taxonomy implies when it identifies "analyzing" as an objective.

7. The taxonomy identifies a large number of different behaviors which may or may not be occurring inside the learner. Whether or not there are actual differences between these behaviors is an open question. What is the difference, for example, between *distinguishing, differentiating,* and *discriminating?* Or what is the difference between *comparing* and *contrasting?* Teachers have spent endless hours arguing about potential differences between certain behaviors. Related to this is another interesting question. How are we to know when the learner stops *comprehending* and starts *applying;* or stops *applying* and starts *analyzing?* These are all internal activities.

The foregoing concerns ultimately need attention from people thinking about and working with instructional objectives. These are difficult and complex concerns, and they are more easily identified than resolved.

What Are Some of the Qualities a Taxonomy of Educational Objectives Should Possess to Be More Functional for Teachers?

You might cast a sigh at this point, asking, If I have difficulty using the presently existing taxonomies and if concerns can be voiced about them, why bother? This is a fair question and a convincing answer has not been forthcoming. Virtually all of the anecdotal data gathered by the author over the past three or four years suggest that taxonomies have not been overly helpful to teachers. Teachers have been doing a rather impressive job generating objectives without them. Still we should probably work for a while at the whole process of generating objectives before drawing conclusions about the ultimate value of taxonomies. Following are some qualities that should improve their usefulness if teachers were to use them.

1. A taxonomy presented to teachers should be able to accommodate behaviors not specifically found in that taxonomy. Provision must be

made for behaviors unique to given areas (e.g., adding, transposing music, hemstitching).

2. A taxonomy should in no way act to limit the behaviors teachers might want to generate on their own.

3. A taxonomy of complete objectives (behaviors and content) would be more useful than a taxonomy of behaviors only.

4. A taxonomy should probably do more than simply describe a group of objectives. It might also prescribe a course of action, for example, suggesting additional objectives or changes in already constructed objectives of guidelines for developing instruction. A taxonomy should be able to do more for teachers than simply provide them with a group of pigeonholes.

5. The establishment of "domain" needs to be reexamined. There are few behaviors which clearly fit into one domain or another. In an attempt to provide a more realistic picture, several different attempts have been made to develop overlapping and continuous domains; these have been little more successful than separate domains. Perhaps the whole notion of "domains" needs to be dropped.

6. Taxonomies should be more involved with classifying overt behavioral tasks that can be performed by the learner and less involved with classifying internal processes which cannot be observed.

7. A taxonomy should be neither very general and loose nor very specific and detailed. General taxonomies tend to be less functional, and specific taxonomies include so much as to render them unwieldy. If a taxonomy is overly structured and detailed, it will tend to harness teachers and hinder more than help them. On the other hand, if it is too general and vague, it will provide little, if any direction and will be discarded by the teacher.

Figures 6 and 7 (on pp. 105–106) represent modified taxonomies, developed by the author and tried out in various teacher workshops. Both of them represent taxonomies of complete objectives; that is, both are designed to contain behaviors and content.

Suggestions for the Teacher Emerging from This Area of Concern

1. You should, for the present, probably spend less time trying to use the Bloom-Group Taxonomies and more time simply generating desired objectives.
2. If a taxonomy is less helpful or less functional for you, do not use one. You need not feel that all or even some of your objectives must come from a taxonomy.
3. You should use a taxonomy rather than letting it use you. Do not allow a taxonomy to force you into developing unwanted objectives.

Figure 6. Modified Taxonomy for Generating Instructional Objectives

| Topics | Covert Behaviors | | | | Overt Behavioral Form | Complete Instructional Objective |
Examples	Predominantly Cognitive	Predominantly Motor	Predominantly Affective	Predominantly Interpersonal		
Constitution	Memorize		Attend			
Interpersonal relationships	Differentiate		Comply			
Short story	Perform a mental sequence		Feel satisfaction			
Paragraph	Conceptualize		Be interested			
The raven	Apply cognitively		Commit			
Arc weld	Analyze					
Voting	Synthesize					
Equations with two unknowns	Evaluate					
Prejudice	Generate					
Bach						
Fur-bearing animals						
Sources of energy						

Figure 7. Modified Taxonomy for Generating Instructional Objectives (Cognitive Only)

Hierarchy of Cognitive Behaviors	Content of the Curriculum		
	Specific Information (Facts)	Concepts	Principles
Memorize (Associate)	As a learning product, student is able to reproduce[1] specific bits of information in an unaltered form.	As a learning product, student is able to reproduce concept definition in an unaltered form.	As a learning product, student is able to reproduce principle statements in an unaltered form.
Differentiate (Discriminate)	As a learning product, student is able to differentiate[2] between and among specific bits of information.	As a learning product, student is able to differentiate between and among definitions of various concepts.	As a learning product, student is able to differentiate between and among statements of principles.
Conceptualize (Abstract-Generalize)		As a learning product, student is able to classify[3] examples and nonexamples of a concept.	As a learning product, student is able to classify examples and nonexamples of a principle.
Apply (Transfer)		As a learning product, student is able to apply[4] concept in novel and appropriate situations.	As a learning product, student is able to apply principle in novel and appropriate situations.

Other: Behaviors in this category include creating, thinking critically, problem solving, evaluating, analyzing, interpreting, extrapolating, etc., and any cognitive behaviors not falling into categories above.

Synonym Behaviors:
[1]List, Recite, Recall
[2]Compare, Contrast, Point out differences
[3]Sort, Choose
[4]Transfer

As such, you might generate desired objectives and *then* use a taxonomy for classifying purposes.

4. You should not be overly concerned about those generated objectives that do not fit into some taxonomy.

5. You should not spend much time trying to decide whether generated objectives fit at one level or another, or into one "domain" or another.

6. You should spend more time "outside" the student where you can hear and see what he is doing, and less time trying to decide what is going on "inside" the student.

7. You should not spend too much time trying to make fine distinctions between covert behaviors presumably taking place inside the student. For example, you should spend little time worrying about whether *contrasting* and *comparing* are the same or different internal behaviors.

Area of Concern Sixteen:
What Does Research Say
About the Use of Instructional Objectives?

You may wonder why research into instructional objectives should be an area of concern. If so many teachers are writing instructional objectives, and if there is so much verbal testimony about their importance, why do we need additional justification for their use, and why should we turn to research for that justification?

With federal monies being poured into education now and over the past several years, and with greater pressure being placed upon educators by the public for instant educational reforms, there has arisen the practice of educational fadism—that is, setting aside the old and adopting the new. "Change!" has been the evangelical cry among educators. This particular brand of change has required innovation, try-out, adoption of new techniques, new materials, and new philosophies about education. With alarming frequency, however, these changes have been ill conceived, hurriedly implemented, and seldom evaluated. After a period of time, some of them die of disenchantment, while others become firmly embedded in current educational practice.

Educational fadism is engaged in for a wide variety of reasons. Some changes are made in the schools solely because the school district down the road has adopted a new practice, and one does not want to be left out. Other changes are made because they are believed to be beneficial to the students. Still others are instigated by sagging finances. For whatever reasons, fadism has generally served to fatigue teachers, produce far too little change in students, and dim the judgment of more than a few educators.

Will educators look back on the current enthusiasm for instructional objectives as but one of many expensive and unfruitful innovations during the sixties and seventies? What is the difference between an educational fad and a permanent, useful change in educational beliefs and practice? Perhaps the major difference is that a fad dies out after an original period of sparkle and enthusiasm, whereas a systematic contribution molds and expands educational practice over a sustained period of time. What will instructional objectives ultimately become? This question is difficult to answer. An educational fad usually dies of disenchantment or neglect resulting from failure to produce demonstrable changes in students. That is, if over a period of time an innovation does not produce clear differences between students using it and those not using it, then the innovation is likely to be discarded. (Unfortunately, however, too many innovations which have failed to produce differences have been retained.)

If instructional objectives, as we now talk about them, are to be finally discarded as an educational fad, we need not wait for the test of time. We can now be about the business of conducting our own evaluation in a systematic way. If, after a series of careful and repeated studies in which the use of instructional objectives is explored in a variety of different ways, we cannot demonstrate some important differences between those students and teachers who use instructional objectives and those who do not, then we have sped up the process of burial in the graveyard of educational fads.

In Area of Concern 5, we provided seven justifications for the use of instructional objectives (see pp. 27–34). These are based upon survey reports and anecdotal observations, not upon carefully controlled research. Additionally, none of these justifications indicated there would be better learning on the part of the student. Simply stated, Will students who use instructional objectives learn better than those who do not use them? This question has to do with the relationship between two classes of variables: use of instructional objectives and better learning.

We need to turn to research and/or evaluation studies to obtain at least a partial answer to the above question. Before doing this, however, let us identify some of the difficulties that arise when such a question is handed to the educational researcher.

First of all, the researcher will ask, What is to be meant by "better learning"? Solving different kinds of problems? Longer retention of rote material? Reduction of learning time? Higher scores on tests measuring conceptual understanding? Changes in attitudes? Whatever constitutes "better learning," it must be clearly defined and measurable.

A second difficulty can best be identified through describing a simple study the researcher might conduct. This study is designed to gather information for the question posed above: Will using instructional objectives produce better learning than not using them?

Suppose we have access to 180 fifth-grade children. They are randomly assigned into six groups of thirty children each. Three groups are labeled instructional-objectives groups, and three, control groups. (By using three of each, we are able to replicate a simple study three times in one study.) Next, we select six teachers matched as much as possible in characteristics (e.g., years of teaching experience, areas of competence) that could affect students' scores on the test. These teachers are then randomly assigned to the six different groups. Suppose we are able to have the teachers perform essentially the same way using the same materials in all groups so that the major difference among the groups is that three have received and used instructional objectives and three have

not. Since the students were initially randomized, a test will be administered at the end of instruction only.

Suppose we define "better learning" as a high score on a test designed
to measure the instructional objectives used in our study; suppose these
objectives cover several units in history. After instruction, this test is
administered to all six groups, and a mean score is obtained for each
group. Among other things, we compare the means of the instructional-
objectives groups with those of the control groups.

Suppose those students receiving instructional objectives scored
significantly higher than those who did not. Do we simply conclude at
this point that using instructional objectives produces better learning
than not using them? Perhaps, but let us look more carefully at the
results. Suppose we notice that the instructional-objectives groups spent
almost twice as much time studying as did the control groups. Furthermore, the mean test scores for the instructional-objectives groups were
considerably higher than those of the control groups. Could the *amount
of study time,* either in addition to or as part of using instructional
objectives, have produced the higher scores? Suppose also, upon further
scrutiny, we note that students in the instructional-objectives groups not
only study longer than those in the control groups, but also review
differently and often read different materials. What effect could *type of
review* and *nature of materials* have in producing higher scores?

We can see from these hypothetical results that "using instructional
objectives" involves several different activities. Any one or a combination
of these specific activities might produce the "better learning." Also, it is
likely that some of these activities produce a greater impact than others;
suppose the type of review turned out to be a rather powerful variable and
was most responsible for the differences in test scores. The difficulty
comes in not being able to tell exactly what brought about the differences, only that there were some. Someday, most of these more specific
variables, all part of "using instructional objectives," will have been
studied both separately and in combination. By then, our conclusions
might have to be qualified. Rather than saying, for instance, that using
instructional objectives produces better learning than not using them, we
might suggest less sweeping and more specific conclusions like: If young
children are the students, if greater retention is desired, and if simple
tasks are used, then using instructional objectives will be more effective
than not using them. Or if the subject matter is rather complex and it is to
be learned by college-age students, then carefully sequenced instructional objectives will be more effective in producing *application* than will
randomly sequenced objectives or no objectives at all. Or instructional
objectives will be more effective in producing intellectual outcomes than
in producing attitude changes, especially with older students. Thus, a
second difficulty encountered is in never being able to make sweeping
and inclusive statements about the effectiveness of instructional objectives. Even if research does find them effective, it will be in certain

learning situations, with certain types of students, and with particular learning outcomes. So, when the educator asks whether using instructional objectives produces better learning than not using them, the question is too inclusive to be meaningful.

A third difficulty in attempting to answer the above question through research is that, in most studies, the cards are stacked in favor of instructional objectives. Suppose the objectives used in our hypothetical study were very specific, bordering on drill objectives. We found out in an earlier discussion that if objectives are specific enough they become the actual evaluation. For example, consider "The student will be able to identify the four parts of a plant." What is the evaluation? Simply a recopying of the objective. With this in mind, the research question we all too often end up asking is, Will a group of students receiving the evaluation prior to and during instruction score higher on that evaluation than students who have not received it? Such a comparison seems unfair. How could those not receiving the objectives (evaluation) possibly do as well as those who have the test and study for it? There is no reason to believe there would *not* be a difference.

These are three of the more obvious difficulties that arise in attempting to conduct research on educational objectives. They have been discussed to enable you to interpret more accurately the research studies to follow.

Research on Instructional Objectives

Like so many other areas of learning and education, there has been relatively little research conducted in the area of instructional objectives. We will take a brief and simplified look at a few of the studies published which are directly concerned with the use of instructional objectives.

Walker (1970) conducted a quasi study in which he classified various goal statements into categories which presumably varied from those that were rather abstract (providing little direction) to those that were mostly concrete (providing considerable direction). These were goal statements about a project on which a group of staff members had been working. The goal statements were randomly presented to the staff members, and they were asked to judge them as to how helpful each would be in introducing a new member to the project. Staff members reported that the goal statements which were most similar to instructional objectives would be most helpful. This study simply suggests that a group of staff members felt that goal statements which were specific and concrete would be more helpful than goal statements which were more abstract and offered less direction.

Baker (1969) selected five general educational objectives in the field of social science. From each of these, she generated four or more specific instructional objectives, making a total of twenty-three. She had three different treatment conditions.

> Treatment 1: A group of experts selected the one instructional objective from each of the five general objectives which they thought best facilitated the learning of all the objectives within that category.
> Treatment 2: A specific instructional objective was randomly selected from those in each category (rather than being selected by a group of experts).
> Treatment 3: This group simply received the five general educational objectives with no specific instructional objectives.

All three groups were tested on items designed to measure the twenty-three instructional objectives that had been generated. Eighteen teachers were randomly assigned to these three treatment groups. Each teacher was asked to teach for the five objectives. In treatment 1, the objectives were instructional objectives and had been selected by a group of experts. In treatment 2, the objectives were instructional objectives and had been selected at random; and in treatment 3, the objectives were educational objectives. The students in these three groups showed no differences in their test scores. One possible conclusion is that using instructional objectives produced no better learning than not using instructional objectives. A second, and probably more feasible conclusion is that we cannot really tell what happened because those teachers who were assigned to use instructional objectives may not, in fact, have used them. Baker does provide some evidence to suggest this as a possible explanation.

Cook (1970) was interested in the following type of question: If students are given instructional objectives along with a unit of instruction, will they show greater learning and less forgetting than a group of students with the same instruction who are not presented with the instructional objectives? There were four groups of elementary education majors who received self-instructional materials covering a mathematical unit of instruction. Group 1 was the control group and was simply given the self-instructional materials with nothing else. Group 2 was given the objectives for each activity in the unit. Group 3 was given the learning sequence at the beginning and at the end of the unit but did not receive any objectives. Group 4 was given both the objectives and the learning sequence. The instruction occurred over eight consecutive days. A posttest was given immediately after the instruction; a retention test, some two weeks later. In general, the results showed no differences among the four groups on the immediate posttest. That is, those students receiving objectives did not perform in a superior way to those not receiving the objectives. However, after two weeks, the group given objectives before each activity in the unit outperformed the other three groups on the retention test. Since one of the other three groups was given objectives, the results become a little confusing at this point. The general results do suggest, however, that those students receiving instructional objectives did not outperform those not receiving them.

Oswald (1970) used 619 students from the eleventh grades in two different schools. Each student was presented with a packet of social studies materials. Additionally, each packet contained the following: (1) It either contained an instructional objective or it did not; (2) if it did contain an instructional objective, it contained one that was either general or specific; and (3) it measured either knowledge or comprehension. Finally, each student received a set of readings and twenty-five multiple-choice questions based exclusively on those readings. Students were given twenty-five minutes to work on the packet and were then immediately given a posttest. One week later they were given the same posttest to check retention. In general, the results showed that those students receiving instructional objectives did not demonstrate a higher performance than those not receiving an instructional objective. Likewise, there were no differences found in comprehension objectives as compared with knowledge objectives, nor between general objectives and specific objectives, either on the posttest or on the retention test.

Jenkins & Deno (1969) conducted a study on the effects of different types of objectives and also the effects on those who received them. They randomly assigned 112 college students to one of six experimental groups and one control group. All of the experimental groups received either a general educational objective or a specific instructional objective. Additionally, the objectives were given either to (1) teachers only, (2) teachers and students, or (3) students only. The control group was neither taught by a teacher nor given any study materials. They simply took the posttest. The students were presented with a unit in social studies and after the instructional period were presented with the final exam. In general, the results showed there were no significant differences among groups receiving general educational objectives, specific instructional objectives, or no objectives. Likewise, there were no differences among the three groups in which the objectives were given to the teachers, to both the teachers and the students, and to the students only.

What Do These Few Studies Tell Us?
First, the research so far in this area is scanty indeed. There has been too little research conducted to draw any serious conclusions about the effectiveness of instructional objectives. Second, we need more research which carefully controls extraneous variables. More simply stated, we need research which helps us sort out what is and what is not at work

when we use instructional objectives. For example, does the degree of specificity of the objective make a difference; does the amount of experience a student has had in using instructional objectives make a difference; does the commitment of the teacher to objectives make a difference; etc.? Third, taken as a group, the above studies do not show that students using instructional objectives learn more than students not using them.

Obviously, as educational researchers, we need to roll up our sleeves and go to work in this area. A great many people are currently expressing enthusiasm for and commitment to the use of objectives, but there is little research to back up such enthusiasm. We need to spend less time proselyting and more time testing the effects of instructional objectives. Following is a list of research questions which need immediate exploration. Systematic research in these areas could provide a more sound basis for either continuing our enthusiasm or making some full-scale alterations in our thinking.

Research Questions in the Area of Instructional Objectives

1. How does the level of specificity of an objective influence its attainment? Are specific objectives attained more easily than less-specific objectives?
2. Does a difficult and complex objective have to be stated more specifically than a less-complex one?
3. Do students who fully participate in the selection of instructional objectives attain them more readily than students who do not?
4. What are the variables which determine whether or not students will use objectives if they are made available to them?
5. What are the variables which determine whether or not teachers will use their objectives to generate instruction and evaluation?
6. How do characteristics (e.g., age, sex, ability, working speed) of students influence their achievement of various types of objectives (e.g., simple, complex)?
7. How similar are the hierarchies of objectives formed by scholars to the hierarchies that would be formed by the students themselves?
8. Do a greater percentage of students achieve an objective if a variety of instructional experiences is provided as compared with only one or two instructional experiences?
9. What are some variables which increase the retention of an achieved objective?
10. What are the criteria teachers typically select to determine the achievement of an objective?
11. How does the use of instructional objectives influence "incidental learning tendencies" of learners? Does their use decrease incidental learning on the part of students?

12. Would students tend to generate objectives similar to those generated by their teacher for a particular unit of instruction?
13. What are the effects of overlearning a set of objectives?
14. To what extent does presenting students with instructional objectives before and during their learning influence their style of learning?
15. What are the effects of sequencing objectives in various orders for a given subject-matter area?
16. What role does past experience in using objectives play in the degree to which instructional objectives will facilitate student learning?
17. Are some methods for generating instructional objectives more timesaving and systematic than others?
18. Are some strategies for deriving instruction from objectives more effective than others?
19. Can teachers acquire a set of measurable and appropriate objectives more effectively by generating their own or by selecting them from other sources?
20. What is the extent of added work involved in developing unique objectives for each student in the class as opposed to having the same objectives for all students in the class?
21. What are the most frequently used criteria in determining the appropriateness of an objective?

Suggestions for the Teacher Emerging from This Area of Concern

1. At least for the present, you should probably try to justify the use of instructional objectives on some other grounds than findings from research.
2. Whenever possible, you should conduct your own research on the effectiveness of instructional objectives.

Epilogue

The objectives for this book were that you would come away with (1) greater confidence in the potential impact of instructional objectives on teaching, (2) knowledge of specific areas with which you must concern yourself if you are to actually use instructional objectives, and (3) some working suggestions for implementing instructional objectives in your teaching.

Now in these last paragraphs, let us seek perspective. The process we call "teaching," when examined under a microscope, turns out to be a rather messy-looking affair. Much of it is intuitive, unstudied, and without serious precision. Additionally, much of the criticism leveled against teaching has also been unstudied and inarticulate. Thus, as educators, we frequently find ourselves in the frustrating position of being unable to carefully describe what it is we do when we teach and, at the same time, unable to seriously modify our teaching behavior because of the fuzzy and inexact criticism of our activities.

It is crucial that we make more precise the process of teaching. But where should precision be imposed? Up until now, what little has existed can be found in preparing and presenting instruction. Much more precision is needed in another area, namely, the relationship between what teachers do and what results occur in the learners. This book has been about that need for more precise identification and measurement of results in students, the student outcomes.

What about making more precise *all* student outcomes? If this be our commitment, what of those gentle and desirable outcomes that elude measurable identification? Are they to be discarded or bent out of shape through forced description as observable behaviors? Should some of these best be left imprecise? Should some suffer from unmeasurability but show strength in being real?

In our enthusiasm for the improvement of teaching, in our well-meaning innovations, and in our increasing commitment to make teaching more scientific, we must be deliberate, sensitive, and careful. We are not justified in destroying that which we are trying to improve. If in our zeal for the use of instructional objectives we manage to eliminate delicate and subtle student outcomes which resist observable definition, we will have moved backward rather than forward. It is obvious, even from preliminary data gathered, that we can quickly shift from too little precision to too much precision . . . and in one large jump. We must be careful not to be guilty of overcompensation because of inexpertise and impatience.

We should attempt to increase the precision of whatever it is we call "teaching" by making more precise *some* student outcomes; at the same time, we should have the maturity to realize there are other student outcomes which will never lend themselves to precise definition but which are still very important and ought to be respected and sought after also. Rejecting outcomes that cannot be precisely identified is just as immature as rejecting precision as a means of improving teaching. Teachers who continually work at becoming more precise in identifying and evaluating student outcomes and are, at the same time, able to value and teach for nonmeasureable outcomes might well be called "effective" teachers.

Appendix A:
Condensed Version of the Text

Area of Concern One:
How Shall We Define an *Objective?*

Any objective (whether a "behavioral" objective or not) should contain the following characteristics:

1. A statement about the learner, not the teacher;
2. The learner's behavior;
3. The topic at which the learner's behavior is directed;
4. The consequences of the learning experience, not the experience itself.

An objective is not a statement about a teacher's intentions or instruction but rather a statement about what the student will have learned. This book considers a *behavior* to be any activity engaged in by the learner whether it can be directly observed or not. Thus, both *reciting* and *appreciating* are behaviors; the former is an overt behavior and the latter a covert behavior. Topics are either in the form of subject matter (e.g., poem, the Civil War, fractions) or skills (welding, volleying, typing). An example of a learning experience is "going to the dairy"; an example of a consequence of that learning experience is "an understanding of where milk comes from."

For specific suggestions to teachers, see page 7.

Area of Concern Two:
How Do Objectives Differ from Each Other?

Objectives differ from each other in many ways, one of which is in their form. Some objectives are more general and others more specific. Additionally, these same objectives are either more overt (observable) or more covert (unobservable).

If an objective is either mostly general or mostly covert or both, it is called an *educational* objective. If an objective becomes specific enough and overt enough so a teacher can teach it and measure its attainment, it qualifies as an *instructional* objective. Finally, if an objective becomes so specific and detailed that no more specific objectives can be generated from it, it is a *drill* objective. Teachers should strive to develop mostly instructional objectives.

For specific suggestions to teachers, see page 11; for examples of educational, instructional, and drill objectives, see Appendix B.

Area of Concern Three:
How Are Objectives Related to Each Other?

Objectives are related to each other (1) through the process of generation and (2) through sampling and inference.

If two or more specific objectives are created from a larger objective, *downward generation* has occurred. If several specific objectives are used to create a more general objective, *upward generation* has occurred. Thus, one objective is related to another as "parent" to "offspring."

For most parent objectives, an infinite number of offspring or more specific objectives *could be* generated. In practice, however, a teacher generates only a representative sample of all those that might be generated. Thus, the relationship of objectives is between those objectives that are generated by the teacher and those that might have been generated.

If a student is able to attain a sample of overt behavioral objectives, the teacher *infers* that the student has also attained a more general covert objective. Stated differently, the teacher uses the attainment of overt objectives as evidence for the attainment of an unmeasurable covert objective.

For specific suggestions to teachers, see pages 17–21.

Area of Concern Four:
How Are Objectives Generated
for an Entire Unit?

Two methods of generating objectives are described in this section. They have been helpful to teachers when used separately or in combination.

Topic Display Method

As a first step, all possible topics that might be taught are gathered together and written down; these are as specific as possible. They are then ordered or sequenced as they are to be taught. The next step is to combine student behaviors with the topics, thereby creating objectives; only those behaviors are used which are considered important by the teacher. Sometimes several topics will be consolidated into one objective, and sometimes several different objectives will be generated from the same topic.

Downward Generation Method

Broad and important educational objectives are written down, and then increasingly more specific objectives are generated from them. (See figure 1 on p. 13.) This occurs until a "network" of objectives has been formulated. Each offspring objective is linked to some parent objective; this parent then becomes an offspring of a more general parent objective. Next, some objectives are re-arranged, others added, and others modified until a satisfying set emerges.

These two methods differ in that with the topic display method specific objectives are generated from a set of topics; with the downward generation method, specific objectives are generated from general objectives.

For specific suggestions to teachers, refer to the methods themselves on pages 22–25.

Area of Concern Five:
Why Have Instructional Objectives?

Following are some justifications for the use of instructional objectives:

1. The teacher will have a method by which to measure, at least partially, important objectives not measured in the past.
2. The teacher and the student will have greater visible evidence that the objectives have been achieved.
3. The student will experience considerably more freedom in achieving an objective.
4. The student will feel greater focus and direction on what is important, on what to study for, and on what he will be evaluated.
5. In the long run, both the teacher and the student will save time and energy.
6. The student will participate more in his own instruction.
7. The teacher will feel greater security with this more direct evidence of "teaching effectiveness."

For specific suggestions to teachers, refer to page 35.

Area of Concern Six:
How Does the Use of Instructional Objectives Differ from What Teachers Have Been Doing All Along?

There are several differences between an instructional-objectives teaching pattern and a more traditional teaching pattern. First, what teachers have been calling "objectives" are not really objectives. They are either statements of topics to be covered (e.g., the earth and its features) or statements of teacher intentions (e.g., to show how clay is thrown on a potter's wheel); neither of these is a legitimate objective.

A second difference is that an instructional-objectives approach places greater emphasis on objectives and on a clear relationship between objectives and instruction. Objectives are generated first and *then* used to prescribe instructional materials and experiences. With the more traditional teaching patterns, objectives are "in the back of the mind" but are seldom used to suggest instruction; indeed, planning of instruction has been the initial rather than the second step.

A third difference is that an instructional-objectives approach places greater emphasis on evaluation and on a clear relationship between objectives and evaluation. Evaluation is seen as an integral part of the teaching process; its major function is to provide feedback for instruction. In the more traditional pattern, evaluation is something tacked on at the end mainly for the purpose of grading; it is seldom used to provide feedback about instruction.

A final difference is that an instructional-objectives approach places greater emphasis on a clear interrelationship between objectives, instruction, and evaluation. All three receive feedback from each other. Since this relationship is seldom clear or tied down in the more traditional pattern, the elements themselves are not effectively used in providing helpful feedback to each other.

For specific suggestions to teachers, refer to page 40.

Area of Concern Seven:
How Useful Are General Educational Objectives?

General educational objectives can be effectively used in the following ways:

1. General objectives provide guidelines for generating a group of related specific objectives.
2. General objectives can provide the relevance for specific instructional objectives; that is, the relevance of any specific objective can be determined by tracing it back through the more general objectives from which it was generated.
3. General objectives provide the teachers with a more encompassing and complete picture of their efforts and thereby prevent them from unintentionally omitting desirable instructional objectives not readily apparent.
4. General objectives facilitate communication with nonprofessional people.
5. The values of society and the community, as well as their priority, are more easily incorporated into general educational objectives than they are into specific instructional objectives.

For specific suggestions to teachers, refer to page 45.

Area of Concern Eight:
Have I Generated Measurable Objectives?

Classifying objectives as "behavioral" or "nonbehavioral" is not very helpful for at least three reasons. First, to say that an objective is "nonbehavioral" does not tell us what it is, but only what it is not. It is not a behavioral objective. Second, we are mistakenly led to believe that all objectives fall neatly into one of two categories. This is simply not the case. There are many objectives which are partly behavioral and others which are partly nonbehavioral. Third, a behavioral objective can quickly turn into a nonbehavioral objective and vice versa. This double classification is confusing to teachers.

Following is a more functional and realistic approach. We enlarge the definition of *behavior* to include not only observable activities of the learner but unobservable ones as well. Thus, since all objectives contain behaviors, they are *all* behavioral objectives. Behavioral objectives differ in their degree of overtness, ranging from highly overt objectives to highly covert objectives. The degree of overtness is determined by the behavior in the context of the objective. A behavior, when placed in one objective, will appear mostly overt; when placed in another objective, that same behavior might appear mostly covert. However, in both cases, it is still a behavior.

Overt behavioral objectives are directly observable and therefore permit measurement. Our ultimate concern is with measurability. What do we measure? We measure differences between behaviors. First, we can measure the differences between a student's present overt behavior and some "ideal" overt behavior stated in an objective. Second, we can measure the difference between a student's initial overt behavior and his changed overt behavior after instruction. Third, we can measure the difference between one student's overt behavior and that of another. When working with objectives we are usually less concerned with this last type of measurement.

For specific suggestions to teachers, refer to page 49.

Area of Concern Nine:
How Appropriate Are My Objectives?

There are two apparent reasons why teachers generate so many unimportant instructional objectives. First, they fail to start out with general educational objectives; second, they simply lack experience and practice in developing objectives which are appropriate.

Following are criteria teachers might use in determining whether or not their instructional objectives are appropriate: (These will not all be used on every objective.)

1. Does the instructional objective seem relevant to the student?
2. Does the instructional objective itself provide any motivation for or is it at least attractive to the student?
3. Is the instructional objective appropriate for the needs of the student?
4. Will the objective be used frequently enough by the student to make its attainment worthwhile?
5. Can the instructional objective be attained by the student within the time allotted?
6. Have each instructional objective's prerequisites been adequately attained?
7. Does the instructional objective specifically prescribe instructional materials and instructional experiences?
8. Are facilities available for the attainment of the instructional objective?
9. Is the instructional objective important enough to justify the staff time and money put in for its attainment?
10. Can the instructional objective be modified or eliminated over time as it becomes more or less important?
11. Can the instructional objective be evaluated satisfactorily?
12. Does a given instructional objective *appear* to be good evidence for the attainment of the educational objective?
13. Is the instructional objective consistent with the teacher's own personal values?
14. Does the instructional objective appear to be consistent with the school's philosophy of education?
15. Is the instructional objective an "in-life" objective, or does it at least contribute to one?
16. Is the instructional objective a prerequisite to later "in-school" objectives?
17. Is the instructional objective appropriate in terms of research results in learning?
18. Is the instructional objective too much like a drill objective?

For specific suggestions to teachers, refer to page 56.

Area of Concern Ten:
How Important Is It to Sequence Objectives in a Given Order?

Surveys show that only a few people have been concerned with the sequencing of behaviors, but a great many people have been concerned with the sequencing of subject matter. Also, very few people have sequenced complete objectives (subject matter and behavior). Teachers need to sequence already-existing objectives as well as those they themselves generate. Following are some suggestions about sequencing:

1. Placing objectives in a particular sequence is most important when the subject matter within the objectives requires a definite sequence.
2. A number of different sequences may work equally well in more areas than we think. Our concern may be exaggerated in some areas and inadequate in others.
3. There are at least two indicators a teacher can use in deciding whether sequencing will be important: (1) As the objectives to be learned become more complex, a particular sequence becomes increasingly important; (2) as the age of the student decreases, the importance of a particular sequence increases.
4. If the objectives have already been constructed, they might be sequenced according to the difficulty of the entire objective, from easiest to most difficult. On the other hand, if the objectives are to be generated, the subject matter might be sequenced first by difficulty or by logical order.
5. Whenever possible, the teacher is encouraged to sequence objectives empirically in terms of their difficulty. This means the teacher presents the class with several different sequences of the objectives and selects the sequence that best facilitates learning.
6. Generally speaking, teachers should impose a sequence on the objectives after they have been generated, not before they are generated.

The above constitute specific suggestions for teachers.

Area of Concern Eleven: How Are Objectives Used in the Planning of Instruction?

Teachers have not as yet made systematic use of instructional objectives in planning instruction for at least three reasons. First, teachers are just now arriving to the point where they are ready to begin trying them out in actual instruction; most of the time up until now has been spent identifying and writing objectives. Second, people writing about instructional objectives have been far more concerned with telling teachers that objectives are good things to have than showing how they might be used. Third, many objectives have been generated in such a specific and detailed form as to render them less useful in the classroom.

Because of the tremendous variation in teaching styles, personalities, backgrounds, etc., teachers are not likely to adopt some common method for deriving instruction from objectives. Furthermore, teachers who have been generating objectives in the most suitable form (instructional rather than educational or drill) have experienced little if any difficulty in using them to plan instruction. The *form* of an objective rather than the particular strategy seems to be the crucial factor in using them to plan instruction.

Following are two orientations that may prove helpful regardless of the methods teachers use to develop instruction from their objectives:

1. Objectives should be thought of as prescribers of instruction rather than as fallouts from instruction. Objectives possess most of their power if generated *prior* to instruction. If they have to be continually teased out of already-existing instruction, this directing power is unused. The more specific an objective becomes the more clearly it prescribes instruction.
2. Attempts should be made to develop "valid" instruction. This means there should be a correspondence between what is covered in the objectives and what is covered in the instruction.

As objectives become increasingly specific, thereby more clearly prescribing instruction, the validity of the instruction can be more easily ascertained.

For specific suggestions to teachers, refer to pages 65–66.

Area of Concern Twelve:
How Can I Tell When My Objectives
Have Been Attained?

Measurement refers to that limited activity of gathering and classifying information through the use of a measuring instrument. *Evaluation* is the making of judgments and decisions based upon information gathered from measurement. Teachers need to engage in more systematic and rigorous measurement as they conduct their evaluations.

Any measuring instrument should (1) be valid for the objectives it measures, and (2) have at least some consistency in measuring whatever it measures. The first characteristic means that the behaviors and topics called forth by the measuring instrument should be as similar as possible to those behaviors and topics identified in the objectives. The second characteristic means that a test should be consistent in ranking students over repeated testings, and also that a student's obtained score should closely approximate his "true" score.

In measuring the attainment of an objective, we can compare a student's performance with some "ideal" performance stated in the objectives, or we can compare the student's performance before instruction with his performance after instruction.

How do we determine when a student has "mastered" an objective? We manufacture a sample of items designed to measure a given objective. We allow the student's performance on this sample to *stand for* his performance on all the items that could have been manufactured to measure that objective. Thus, if he correctly answers 90% of the items in the sample, we say he could also correctly answer 90% of all possible items measuring the objective. We can also say that he has achieved 90% of the objective because our items have been selected as measures of the objective.

To what degree do students need to achieve an objective in order to "master" it? This level is established arbitrarily by the teacher. In measuring an objective, we need to know both to what *degree* the objective has been achieved and also whether or not this degree constitutes "mastery" or "nonmastery."

When grading instructional objectives, we should generally compare the student's performance to some standard, not to the performance of other students. We can grade the student both on the degree to which the objectives have been achieved and whether or not they indicate mastery or nonmastery.

For specific suggestions to teachers, refer to page 85.

Area of Concern Thirteen: What Effects Do Instructional Objectives Have on Individual Differences?

Many teachers feel that using instructional objectives will make all the students more alike at a time when they want to teach for greater individual differences among students. This concern requires careful thought. First of all, there are many behaviors and topics in existing curricula in which teachers do not want students to differ. Second, there is always a great deal of confusion about what teachers mean by "individual differences" and "individualized instruction."

Instructional objectives per se have no effect whatsoever on increasing or decreasing individual differences. The *way* an objective is stated, however, does produce very marked effects. An objective can be stated so as to increase individual differences or to decrease them.

Teachers who suddenly switch to the use of instructional objectives find that their students tend to become increasingly different in the speed with which they learn material; at the same time, they tend to become increasingly similar in the extent to which the material is learned.

Teachers can individualize their instruction by (1) having a different set of objectives for each student; (2) having the same objectives for all students but different means for attaining them; (3) creating their own set of personal objectives for their own classes; (4) designating different mastery levels for different students; and (5) providing greater individual pacing within the class.

For specific suggestions to teachers, refer to pages 90–91.

Area of Concern Fourteen: Who Should Be Responsible for Developing Objectives, and What Sources Are Available?

An ever widening circle of people should take on responsibility for the development of objectives. This does not mean that all elements of society should be involved with the development of specific instructional objectives in the classroom, but it does mean that all elements should be represented in suggesting educational objectives.

The student, teacher, principal, district curriculum specialists, visiting personnel, and university professors all have either direct or indirect influence on instructional objectives found in the classroom. In the noneducational community, people like parents, local and federal governments, private industry, and the school board also influence instructional objectives found in the classroom.

People in the educational and noneducational communities outside the immediate classroom should probably lend their attention to generating the more broad educational objectives. People closer to the classroom (e.g., district curriculum committees) should spend most of their efforts in translating educational objectives into general instructional objectives. Finally, the teacher in the classroom and, when appropriate, the student have the major responsibility for generating specific instructional objectives that will be taught. Teachers should be sensitive to educational objectives developed by people outside the classroom; in turn, those outside the classroom should be sensitive to the instructional objectives developed by the teacher.

Most sources for objectives (1) have turned out to be something other than legitimate objectives, (2) have turned out to be educational rather than instructional objectives and have been outdated, or (3) cannot be readily adapted into the teacher's curriculum because they are inappropriate for the teacher's own purposes.

If you are interested in locating examples of *instructional* objectives, two sources are helpful. First, securing instructional objectives developed by other schools or other districts either close by or across the nation is of definite value. Second, the Instructional Objectives Exchange (objectives "bank") has been used with varying degrees of success.

Perhaps the most useful source to which you can turn is your own experience and a wide variety of subject-matter guides (e.g., textbooks, teacher editions, curriculum subject-matter guides).

For specific suggestions to teachers, refer to page 97.

Area of Concern Fifteen:
How Usable Is a Taxonomy
of Educational Objectives?

A taxonomy of educational objectives is a scheme for classifying educational objectives in some particular order. The Bloom-Group Taxonomy has been the most widely discussed authority and source for educational objectives, especially those which are "cognitive" and "affective." Although these taxonomies have purported advantages, teachers—in actual practice—have been largely unsuccessful in attempting to use them. The apparent reasons for this are listed on pages 99–101 of the text. Additional concerns that can be raised about the taxonomies themselves are found on pages 101–103. Finally, a list of qualities a taxonomy of educational objectives should possess in order to be more functional for teachers appears on pages 103–104.

For specific suggestions to teachers, refer to pages 104–107.

Area of Concern Sixteen:
What Does Research Say
About the Use of Instructional Objectives?

The justifications listed in Area of Concern 5 for using instructional objectives are based upon survey reports and anecdotal observations, not upon carefully controlled research. Additionally, none of these justifications indicated there would be "better learning" on the part of students using instructional objectives. A simple research question might be, Will students who use instructional objectives "learn better" than those who do not use them? There are several problems that make a direct and sweeping answer to this question difficult. First, "better learning" can mean a great many different things, and each must be specified. Second, there are factors other than the use of objectives per se which will influence "better learning." For example, the amount of study time, the type of review, and the nature of materials used may be different for students using instructional objectives than for those who do not. Could it be these factors rather than instructional objectives that produce "better learning"? When much more research has been conducted in this area, we can answer the question in specific contexts. For example, future research might indicate that if we have young children, if the tasks are simple, and if greater retention is desired, then using instructional objectives will be more effective than not using them. A third problem hindering research about the effectiveness of instructional objectives is that of "stacking the cards" in favor of the instructional-objectives group. Giving specific objectives is like giving the final exam. The question might well be, Will students who have the final exam prior to and during instruction score higher on that exam than students who have not received it?

The actual research conducted to this point has been scanty indeed. No serious conclusions can be drawn about the effectiveness of using instructional objectives. There are several studies which suggest that students with instructional objectives do not show greater learning than students without them. The safest conclusion at this point is that we need to roll up our sleeves and conduct some telling research. A list of questions that could be profitably explored through careful research appears on pages 114–115.

For specific suggestions to teachers, refer to page 115.

Appendix B:
Examples of Educational, Instructional, and Drill Objectives

Examples of Educational Objectives
General Educational Objectives
The learner will:

Have developed a code of behavior on ethical principles consistent with democratic ideals.

Be able to participate actively as an informed and responsible citizen in solving the social, economic, and political problems of one's community, state, and nation.

Have attained satisfactory emotional and social adjustment.

Have acquired the knowledge and attitudes basic to a satisfying family life.

Have acquired and be able to use the skills and habits involved in critical and constructive thinking.

Have acquired basic skills, learnings, and attitudes which aid clear thought, logical reasoning, and the development of an appreciation of artistic and cultural values.

Recognize that learning about our American democratic society is both a privilege and a responsibility.

Respect the worth and dignity of every individual.

Have learned how to learn, how to attack new problems, how to acquire new knowledge.

Be able to use rational processes in solving problems.

Have developed values from new experiences.

Have built competence in basic skills.

Fully develop unique potentialities.

Have developed an awareness of social phenomena.

More Specific Educational Objectives
The learner will:

Have a knowledge of fractions and their use.

Have a knowledge of proper dental care.

Have a fundamental knowledge about physical skills and stunts in tumbling.

Have a knowledge of foods and their nutritional value.

Have developed a positive self-concept toward other children in the school.

Have developed new concepts of distance, size, time, direction, and motion.

Understand farm animals.

Have an understanding of the selection of clothes according to personality, design, line, and color.

Have a basic understanding of jet and rocket engines.

Have a knowledge of the adjective clause.

Have an understanding of linear equations.

Have an appreciation for the scientific method.

Have an awareness of the causes of the Civil War.

Have an understanding of the process of photosynthesis.

Have an appreciation of the novel as a form of fiction and prose.

Have a knowledge of Norway.

Be able to describe literary forms.

Be able to explain the motivations of modern authors.

Be able to analyze human behavior.

Be able to evaluate the factors that promote progress.

Be able to apply concepts learned in school to day-to-day living.

Be able to translate French into English.

Be able to generate new ideas.

Examples of Instructional Objectives

The learner will:

Be able to identify various kinds of birds, their homes, and their habitats.

Be able to display the proper care and use of tumbling equipment (e.g., moving mats, washing mats).

Be able to explain the rules and terminology of lacrosse; given any specific game situation, correctly identify and apply the appropriate rule.

Be able to define the major terms used in weight training.

Be able to describe the origin of volleyball and trace its development.

In a (1) contrived situation and/or (2) game situation, be able to correctly demonstrate the following skills: Strategy (timing, individual and team strategy, offensive, defensive, placement, and spin), officiating, spin, net recovery, volley, pass (overhead), underhand serve, overhead serve, side-arm serve, set up, bump, dig.

Be able to execute basic techniques of modern dance.

Given a picture of any coin, be able to identify it.

Given a clock, be able to state the time to the nearest minute.

Be able to correctly tell time.

Given an inch ruler, be able to construct a line segment of a specified length designated to the nearest whole inch.

After looking up a word in the dictionary, be able to use it correctly in a sentence.

Be able to organize pertinent information gained for a certain topic.

Be able to correctly use a phonograph.

Be able to predict appropriate outcomes for a story.

Be able to select appropriate titles for a given reading selection (paragraph or story).

Be able to use the three types of cards in the card catalogue to locate a book.

Given a short story with the ending omitted, be able to predict a realistic ending for the story.

Given any word on his level, be able to identify its several meanings.

Given a word, be able to write its synonym.

Given a list of words and a group of objects, be able to match the words with the correct objects.

After reading a story, be able to present an art exhibit by modeling the characters in clay.

Given a poem, be able to interpret its meaning through pantomine.

Given a group of "tall ideas," be able to create a short story from these.

Given a character, time, place, and event, be able to create a short story from these.

Given an encyclopedia on his level, be able to locate information related to a specific topic.

After locating information of a certain subject in a dictionary and in an encyclopedia, be able to compare the differences between the two types of information received.

Given a list of words, be able to alphabetize them by their first letters.

Given a graph on his level, be able to interpret the data by answering questions which involve the use of the graph.

Given a number of objects, be able to organize them according to a given classification.

Be able to recall in sequential order (either orally or in writing) the events in a story.

Be able to read a set of directions and follow them.

Be able to identify each part of a fraction and explain what each represents.

Be able to add and subtract any set of like fractions.

Be able to read both a sentence and a paragraph, using proper inflections.

Be able to answer questions with a complete sentence.

Given a word beginning with a consonant blend, be able to write that blend.

Given words written in both the singular and plural form and a group of incomplete sentences, be able to insert the proper form of the word in the sentence.

Be able to easily and correctly pronounce words in a given list.

Be able to correctly identify long and short vowels.

Be able to correctly identify stem or root words.

Given a specific written sentence, be able to draw a picture to illustrate it.

After observing a tree, be able to locate, sketch, and describe animals or insect signs left on the tree.

Be able to state the main idea of a sentence and a paragraph.

Be able to describe the major factors leading up to the Civil War.

Be able to refrain from making fun of people who are different from oneself.

Be able to correctly perform various sewing procedures.

Examples of Drill Objectives

The learner will.

Given a set of four picture-card words, three beginning with the "m" sound and one beginning with the "d" sound, be able to point to the word that begins with a different sound.

Be able to define *nutrition* as the science which deals with the way in which food is used in the body with respect to health.

Be able to correctly identify a penny, a nickel, and a dime.

Be able to identify the following as examples of jet propulsion: roller-skate demonstration, balloon demonstration, balloon and milk-carton boat demonstration.

Be able to name the distinctive body parts of an insect as six legs, two feelers, and wings.

Be able to write the names of the five heavenly bodies which are in the Universe.

Be able to define *marbling* as the fat which occurs within the muscle of the meat and which influences the tenderness and flavor of meat.

Given the terms *digestion, absorption,* and *metabolism,* be able to briefly describe their function and give the following description of how the processes relate to one another: Digestion involves the process of breaking down food particles by enzymes in the mouth, stomach, and small intestine. The resulting food particles are absorbed from the small intestine and pass into the blood stream or lymphatic system. The absorbed food particles are transported to the cells where carbon dioxide, water, and energy are released as a process of metabolism.

Using mathematical language, be able to define the following six trigonometric functions: *sine, cosine, tangent, cotangent, secant,* and *cosecant.*

Be able to do six push-ups.

Without the aid of notes, be able to define an *adjective clause* as "a dependent clause, introduced by a relative pronoun, which modifies a noun in the independent clause."

Be able to define a *personal-liberty law* as a law of a northern state prohibiting compliance with the Fugitive Slave Act.

On first hearing the telephone ring, be able to answer it promptly.

While extending elbows and flexing fingers and wrists to snap the hit on contact with the ball, be able to correctly receive an overhead volley.

Given pictures of bread, meat, raw carrots, and the inside of the mouth, be able to point to the front teeth and tell that they are used for cutting foods like bread, the intermediate teeth for tearing tougher foods like meat, and the molars for grinding foods like carrots.

Be able to count by two's up to forty.

Be able to count to 100.

Be able to adjust a clarinet reed for optimal response.

Be able to demonstrate the color symbols for land and water by coloring a world or hemisphere map using blue for water and brown for land.

Be able to run a vertical downbead with each of the arc welders and in the shop three out of four trials using mild steel base metal and E 6011 rod.

Be able to produce a sample of a double pointed dart and a curved dart.

Be able to differentiate between milk chocolate and fondant chocolate.

Be able to identify rayon and acetate by means of the acetone test.

Be able to pick up a premarked piece of board and place it on the jigsaw table with the beginning of the line touching the teeth of the jigsaw blade.

Be able to select the table knife and use it correctly in spreading butter on a slice of bread.

Be able to state on paper that the seventh place from the right is the millions place.

Be able to list at least five foods eaten by the Indians living west of the Cascades.

Be able to verbally reproduce short *a.*

Be able to measure a math book, a test paper, and given line segments to the nearest inch.

Appendix C:
Examples of Topic Displays
and Generation Charts

Examples of Method 1

Breaking a Parent Objective Down
into More Specific Behaviors
and Topics (Offspring Objectives)

Example 1

Parent objective
The learner will become aware of similarities and differences between things.

Offspring objectives
The learner will be able to:
1. Discriminate between geometric shapes.
2. Correctly name various colors.
3. Correctly name any letter of the alphabet.
4. Match pictures with words.
5. Identify different sides of the body and explain their relationships.

Example 2

Parent objective
The learner will be able to interpret reading material.

Offspring objectives
The learner will be able to:
1. Write a brief explanation of the facts found in a story.
2. Convey orally or in writing feelings such as sorrow or happiness found in a story.
3. After reading half of a story, predict a possible conclusion to the story.
4. Given headlines, cartoons, quotations, select those which have meanings similar to those found in a story.

Example of Method 2

Using the Shotgun Approach
(Spontaneously Generating Offspring Objectives
from a Single Parent Objective)[1]

Parent objective
The learner will be able to add numbers.

Spontaneously generated offspring objectives
The learner will be able to:

Given several sets, indicate the union of these sets.

Given two disjoint sets, form the union set and state its cardinal number.

Given two disjoint sets of elements, unite the sets numerically by finding the cardinal number of the new set thus formed.

Given an addition problem, construct pictorally the union of its two disjoint sets and write the numerical representation of the union.

Indicate knowledge of basic addition facts to ten using two addends.

Given an addition problem of two addends through sums of eighteen, indicate the sum.

Given an addition problem through sums of eighteen, and given the sum and one addend, indicate the missing addend.

Given two-digit numerals in column addition, find the sum without regrouping.

Given an addition equation with two addends, reverse the order of the addends and find the sum.

Given an addition problem of up to three addends with a sum through eighteen, solve the equation by combining two of the addends in parentheses and adding their sum to the remaining addend.

Given an addition problem of three- and four-digit numerals, indicate the sum.

Given a two-digit numeral addition problem of two addends, with regrouping, indicate the sum.

Given a three-digit numeral addition problem of two addends, write the sum with regrouping.

Given an addition problem with two addends of three to four digits, write the sum.

---

[1]From inservice teacher workshops, Lake Washington Schools, Kirkland,Washington.

Examples of Topic Outlines[2]

Biology

Lab Techniques
  Using the microscope
    Location of the microscope
    Handling of the microscope
    Slide making
    Lab drawings
    Magnification
  Safety measures in the laboratory
    Lighting the Bunsen burner
    Bending and cutting glass tubing
    Proper heating techniques
    Handling chemicals
    Location of materials

Girl's Tennis

Game
  History—origin and development
  Diagram of playing area
  Names and position of players
  Courtesy and sportsmanship
  Equipment
Skills
  Grips
    Western
    Eastern
  Strokes
    Grip
    Body position
    Forehand
    Backhand
    Service
    Volley
    Smash
    Lob
  Footwork

---

[2]These sections have been taken from both unit and entire course outlines; they are from inservice teacher workshops, Federal Way and Castle Rock, Washington.

Woodshop
Lumber
  Classification and Growth
    Comparison of common woods
    Habitat characteristics and uses
      Where grown
      How used
    Plywood
      How made
      Advantages
      Where used

U.S. History
Industrial Progress and Technological Change in the United States
  Trade unions developed through grievances of industrial workers
    Unions which strive to relieve the problems of labor through organized
        efforts
      Knights of Labor
      Industrial Workers of the World
      CIO
      AFL
    Labor workers who came from the ranks to lead the revolution of labor
        unions
      Samuel Gompers
      John L. Lewis
      Eugene Debs
      Uriah Stevens
    Conflicts which broke out between labor and management due to conflicts of
        interest
    Objectives of both labor and management in order to see both sides of the
        question

Traffic-Safety Education
In the Automobile
  Door checks
  Seat adjustment—how and why
    Seat- and shoulder-belt adjustments
  Mirror adjustments—how and why
  Panel and its importance
  Use and importance of equipment
    Ignition
    Brakes
    Vents
    Lights

Shop
Oxyacetylene Welding
  Fusion welding
    Preparing joints for welding
    Making butt welds in steel
    Making fillet welds in steel
  Bronze welding
    Preparing joints for braze welding of steel
    Adjusting the flame and tinning surface
    Adding metal to the weld
  Cutting with the oxyacetylene flame
    Lighting and adjusting the flame
    Cutting steel

Music in the Humanities
Principles of Musical Structure
  General principles
    Theme
    Unity
    Variety
    Contrast
  Simple sectional structures
  Larger sectional forms
  Contrapuntal forms
  Free forms
  Compound structures

Football
Skills
  Catching
  Throwing
  Stances
  Ball Handling
  Blocking
  Offense Plays
  Defense Plays
Rules
Strategy and Play
  Offensive
  Defensive
Participation
Safety

Algebra I
The Integers and Their Properties
  Positive and negative numbers
  Absolute value of a number
  Addition of integers
  Multiplication of integers
  Subtraction of integers
  Division of integers
  Using parentheses with integers
  Powers of negative numbers
  Adding and subtracting like terms
  Multiplying and dividing terms
  Evaluating algebraic expressions

General Homemaking

Foods and Nutrition
  Nutrition principles
    The four basic food groups needed for good health
    Number of servings in each food group for a teen-ager
    Functions of the nutrients in the body
    Meal plans that will satisfy the basic four food groups
    Students' eating habits in relationship to the basic four food groups
  Attractive meals
    Factors that make an attractive meal
    Attractive meals that satisfy requirements of the basic four food groups
  Table service
    Styles of table service
    Table service according to appropriate situations
  Table etiquette
    Principles and importance of table etiquette
    Application of acceptable table etiquette at meals
    Entertaining a guest at a meal using acceptable table etiquette

Spelling

Phonemic Analysis
  Consonants
    Variants
    Silent
  Vowels
    Long
    Short
    Schwa
    Silent
    "l" and "r" controlled vowels
    Diphthongs
    Digraphs
  Word patterns

Fractions
Reducing fractions to lowest terms
Changing improper fractions
Changing mixed numbers to simplest form
Changing a fraction to higher terms
Finding the lowest common denominator and changing fractions to have
    equivalent denominators
Addition of fractions and mixed numbers
Borrowing in subtraction of fractions
Subtraction of fractions and mixed numbers
Comparing fractions
Changing mixed numbers to improper fractions
Multiplication of fractions and mixed numbers
Division of fractions and mixed numbers
Finding what part one number is of another
Finding a number when a fractional part of it is known

Reading (Grade 2)
Word Recognition
  Structural analysis
    Sight words
    Context clues
    Word attack
    Syllabication
    Stem or root words
    Prefix and suffix
    Contractions
    Possessive nouns
    Regular or irregular forms
    Antonyms, synonyms, homonyms, acronyms
  Phonetic analysis
    Beginning, medial, final consonants
    Short and long vowels
    Consonant blends
    Consonant digraphs
    Diphthongs
    Rhyming words

Examples of Generating Objectives from a Topic Display[3]

Example 1: Topic Display

Language Usage
Written Usage
  Punctuation
    Capitalization
    Commas
    Writing dialogue
    Semicolons
    Special punctuation marks
    Titles and headings

Example 1: Instructional Objectives

Capitalization

1. In sentences with no capital letters (except the first word), the student will be able to find and capitalize the following kinds of proper nouns:
   a. "Calendar" nouns
   b. Living things, places
   c. Groups of people
   d. Historical events and documents
2. In sentences with no capital letters (except the first word), the student will be able to find and capitalize the following "capitalization demons":
   a. Proper adjectives
   b. School subjects
   c. Compass directions
   d. Family relations

Commas

1. In sentences with words or phrases in a series, the student will be able to insert the commas.
2. In sentences with no commas, the student will be able to insert commas needed and label one of the following reasons for each comma:
   a. Direct address
   b. Introductory word
   c. Parenthetical expression
   d. Appositive
3. In a paragraph with no commas, the student will be able to insert commas in:
   a. Introductory phrases and clauses
   b. Compound sentences

---

[3] *Ibid.*

Example of a Network of Topics Using a Generation Chart[4]

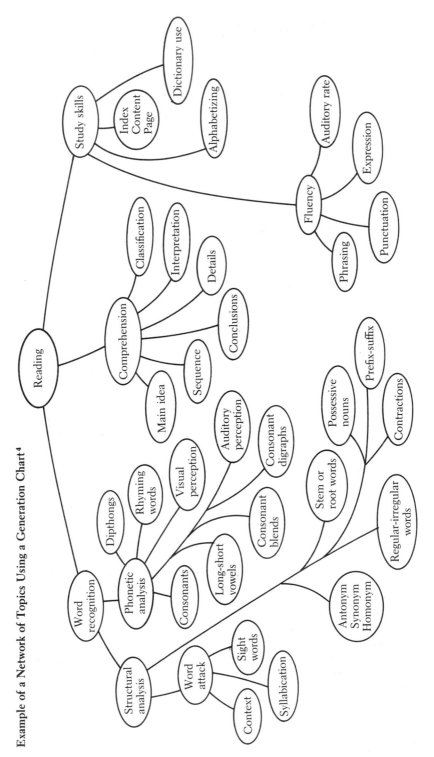

[4]Preliminary sketch taken from inservice teacher workshop, Marysville, Washington.

Example 2: Topic Display

Man and Society

IV. Family
   A. Families everywhere fulfill a few basic and significant functions although ways of living differ from society to society.
   B. Family structure varies.
>   Nuclear, extended, joint
>   Patrilineal, matrilineal, bilateral
>   Role relationships differ in different cultures
   C. Families change
>   The change may be cyclical or long lasting
>   Causes of change
>   Change related to other institutions in society
>   Some factors support the status quo
>   Stereotype
   D. Much of the societal processes found within the larger society are also found in the family.
>   Conflict
>   Competition
>   Domination—Submission
>   Accommodation

Example 2: Instructional Objectives

IV A

The student will be able to:

1. List and explain basic functions families everywhere perform.
2. Compare how these functions are satisfied among different cultures.
3. Explain the family's responsibility in socializing children.
4. Give examples of the way different cultures socialize their children.

IV–B

The student will be able to:

1. Differentiate between the various types of family structures.
2. Explain how family structures impose different role relationships on their members.
3. Differentiate between the various types of family status.
4. Describe family structures in a variety of cultures different from one's own.
5. Compare the family structures and the family roles in a variety of cultures.

Example of a Network of Topics Using a Generation Chart [5]

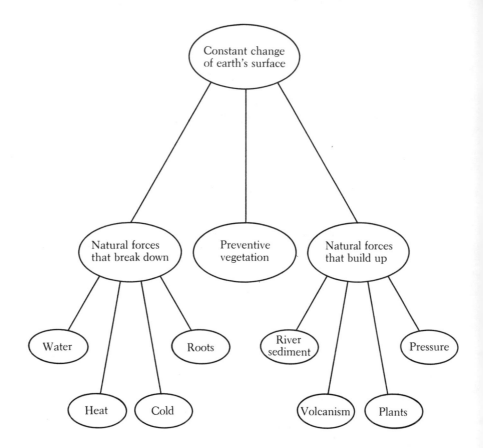

[5]Ibid.

IV–C
The student will be able to:

1. Differentiate between the various types of family changes that occur.
2. Give specific examples of each.
3. Explain the relationship between family change and how it affects other institutions in society.
4. Describe how various factors in society work to maintain traditional family structure and the roles of its members.
5. Predict the changes that will take place within the family during the next fifty years.
6. Judge whether basic functions of the family are being met in various contrived "families."

Example of a Downward Generation Method of Generating Objectives for Reading (Kindergarten through Grade Six) [6]

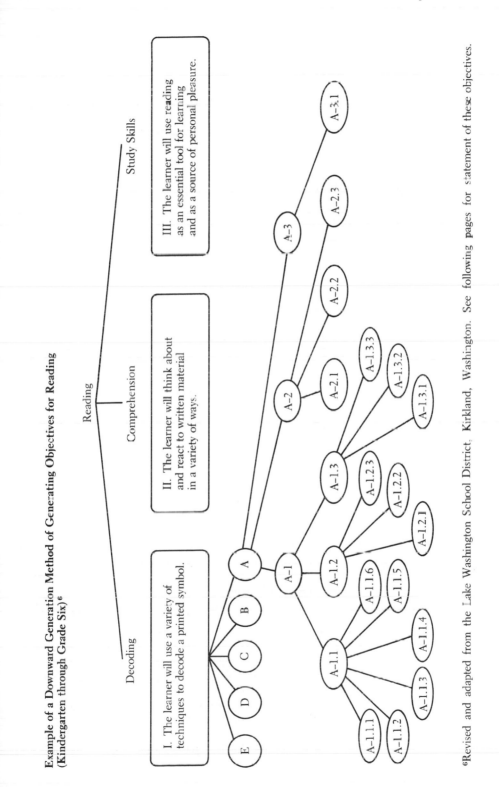

[6]Revised and adapted from the Lake Washington School District, Kirkland, Washington. See following pages for statement of these objectives.

IV–D

The student will be able to:

1. Define various terms related to social processes.
2. Identify examples of conflict, competition, domination, submission, and accommodation in typical family situations.
3. Identify the above processes within the large society.

Examples of Reading Objectives

The learner will be able to:

E. Use the dictionary to decode a printed symbol.
D. Use clues in the context to decode a printed symbol.
C. Use structural analysis to decode a printed symbol.
B. Use phonemic analysis to decode a printed symbol.
A. Use auditory and visual perception preparatory to decoding a printed symbol.

A-3. Associate graphemes with their name.
   A-3.1 Recognize and name all twenty-six graphemes of the alphabet in both upper- and lower-case forms.
A-2. Discriminate visually objects, pictures, shapes, letter forms, and word configurations.
   A-2.3 Distinguish likenesses and/or differences in word configurations.
   A-2.2 Distinguish likenesses and/or differences between upper- and lower-case letter forms.
   A-2.1 Distinguish likenesses and/or differences among objects, pictures, and shapes.
A-1. Discriminate auditorially general sounds, phonemes, and rhyming words.
   A-1.3 Distinguish similarities and/or differences among the sounds of the rhyming elements in words.
      A-1.3.3 Given three words orally, all of which rhyme, pronounce the words and identify them as rhyming words.
      A-1.3.2 Given a list of words orally, two of which rhyme, identify those that rhyme.
      A-1.3.1 Given three words orally, all of which rhyme, pronounce the words and identify them as rhyming words.
   A-1.2 Distinguish similarities and/or differences among phonemes.
      A-1.2.3 Given three picture word cards depicting objects whose names begin with the same phoneme, the learner will identify the objects pictured and tell if they begin with the same phoneme.
      A-1.2.2 Given a list of words orally, pick out the one with a different beginning phoneme.
      A-1.2.1 Given three names orally (Ben, Betty, Mark), the learner will identify the two names that begin with the same phoneme.

A-1.1 Distinguish similarities and/or differences in environmental sounds.

    A-1.1.6 Given sounds in varying rhythmic patterns, reproduce the patterns heard.

    A-1.1.5 After listening to sounds with varying intensity and pitch on instruments, distinguish among these sounds by describing each as loud, soft, high, or low.

    A-1.1.4 After listening to two sounds, one grossly different, tell that the sounds are different.

    A-1.1.3 After listening, with eyes closed, to several loud and soft sounds, identify each sound as being either loud or soft.

    A-1.1.2 After listening, with eyes closed, to familiar sounds from home and school, identify the sound and tell whether it might be heard at school, home, or both.

    A-1.1.1 After listening, with eyes closed, to familiar environmental sounds, identify each one.

Bibliography

Abramson, D. A. Curriculum research and evaluation: Objectives. *Review of Educational Research,* 1966, 36(3), 389–91.

Adler, I. What shall we teach in high school geometry? *The Mathematics Teacher,* 1968, 61(3), March, 226–38.

Advisory Board on Education. *Psychological research in education,* Publication 643. Washington, D.C.: National Academy of Science—National Research Council, 1958, 31.

Ahmann, J. S., & Glock, M. D. *Evaluating pupil growth.* (2nd ed.) Boston: Allyn & Bacon, 1963.

Aiken, W. M. *The story of the eight year study.* New York: Harper & Row, 1942.

American Association of School Administrators. *Imperatives in education.* Washington, D.C.: American Association of School Administrators, 1966.

American Educational Research Association. *Monograph Series on Curriculum Evaluation. Instructional Objectives, 3.* Chicago: Rand McNally, 1969.

Ammerman, H. L. *Development of procedures for deriving training objectives for junior officers.* Alexandria, Virginia: Human Resources Research Office, George Washington University, 1966.

Ammerman, H. L. Some important ways in which performance objectives can vary. Symposium, Human Resources Research Office, George Washington University, Alexandria, Virginia, 1966.

Ammons, M. An empirical study of progress and product in curriculum development. *Journal of Educational Research,* 1964, 27, 451–57.

Ammons, M. The definition, function and use of educational objectives. *Elementary School Journal,* 1962, 62(8), May, 432–36.

Ammons, M., & Gilchrist, R. S. *Assessing and using curriculum content.* A report of the Second National Conference on Curriculum Projects, Chicago, December 1964. Washington, D.C.: Association for Supervision and Curriculum Development, 1965.

Anthony, A. The role of objectives in the "new history." *Social Education,* 1967, 37(7), November, 574–80.

Armstrong, R. J., Cornell, T. D., Kraner, R. E., & Roberson, E. W. *The development and evaluation of behavioral objectives.* Worthington, Ohio: Charles A. Jones, 1970.

Arnstine, D. G. The language and values of programmed instruction: Part 2. *The Educational Forum,* 1964, 28, January, March, 219–26, 337–46.

Arny, C. B. *Evaluation and investigation in home economics.* New York: Appleton-Century-Crofts, 1953, 25.

Atkin, M. J. Behavioral objectives in curriculum design: A cautionary note. *The Science Teacher*, 1968, 35(5), May, 27-30.

Ausubel, D. P. Crucial psychological issues in the objectives, organization, and evaluation of curriculum reform movements. *Psychology in the Schools*, 1967, 4(2), March, 111-21.

Baker, E. Effects on student achievement of behavioral and nonbehavioral objectives. *Journal of Experimental Education*, 1969, 37, 5-8.

Baker, R. L. The educational objectives controversy. Paper presented at the Annual AERA Convention, Chicago, February 1968.

Bauchman, G. D. Education for a continually changing environment. *Journal of Secondary Education*, 1968, 43, April, 156-61.

Bauchman, G. D., & Mayrhofer, A. Leadership training project: A final report. *Journal of Secondary Education*, 1965, 40(8), 369-72.

Beck, J., & Shaw, W. A. Learning and teaching: An analysis and characterization. *Psychological Review*, 1960, 7(3), December, 543-53.

Berg, H. D. *Evaluation in social studies. Thirty-fifth yearbook of the National Council for Social Studies.* Washington, D.C.: National Education Association, 1965.

Berger, E. The development of an information system for elementary school mathematics curriculum materials. Report prepared by the Bureau of Research and the Bureau of General and Academic Education of the Pennsylvania Department of Public Instruction, November 1967.

Bernabei, R. Logical analysis of achievement tests. Unpublished doctoral dissertation, Western Reserve University, Ohio, 1966.

Bialek, H. M. A measure of teachers' perceptions of Bloom's educational objectives. Paper presented to the Annual AERA Convention, New York, February 1967. (Mimeographed)

Bloom, A. M. Inward look. *American School and Universities*, 1964, 37, December, 11.

Bloom, B. S. Learning for mastery. *Evaluation Comment*, 1968, 1(2).

Bloom, B. S., Engelhart, M. D., Furst, E. J., Hill, W. H., & Krathwohl, D. R. *Taxonomy of educational objectives (The classification of educational goals), Handbook 1: Cognitive domain.* New York: David McKay, 1956.

Bobbitt, F. Curriculum-making in Los Angeles. *Supplementary Educational Monographs.* Chicago: University of Chicago Press, 1922, No. 20, 106.

Bobbitt, F. *How to make a curriculum.* Boston: Houghton Mifflin, 1924, 292.

Bonds, A. B., Jr. Education for wisdom. *National Association of Secondary School Principals*, 1966, 50, April, 147-53.

Brackenbury, R. Guidelines to help schools formulate and validate objectives. *Rational planning in curriculum and instruction.* Washington, D.C.: National Education Association, 1967.

Bradfield, J. M., & Moredock, H. S. *Measurement and evaluation in education.* New York: Macmillan, 1957, Chap. 2.

Brothers, A., & Holsclaw, C. Fusing behavior into spelling. *Elementary English*, 1969, 46(1), January, 25-28.

Bruner, J. S. Education as social invention. *Saturday Review*, 1966, 49(8), February 19, 70-72.

Bryan, J. F., & Locke, E. A. Goal setting as a means of increasing motivation. *Journal of Applied Psychology*, 1967, 51, 274-77.

Bryan, J. F., & Locke, E. A. Parkinson's law as a goal setting phenomenon.

Organizational Behavior and Human Performance, 1967, 2, 258–75.

Bull, M. A comparison of goal-setting behavior of achieving and underachieving elementary school boys and their parents. *Dissertation Abstracts,* 1966, 27, 961.

Burns, R. W. Measuring objectives and grading. *Educational Technology,* 1968, 8(18), 13–15.

Burns, R. W. Objectives and classroom instruction. *Educational Technology,* 1967, 7(17), September 15, 1–3.

Burns, R. W. Objectives and content validity of tests. *Educational Technology,* 1968, 8(23), 17–20.

Burns, R. W. Objectives involving attitudes, interests, and appreciations. *Educational Technology,* 1968, 8(8).

Burns, R. W. The practical educational technologist: Objectives in action. *Educational Technology,* 1968, 8(3), February 15, 14–15.

Burns, R. W. The theory of expressing objectives. *Educational Technology,* 1967, 7(20), October 30, 1–3.

Burr, J. B., Harding, L. W., & Jacobs, L. B. *Teaching in the elementary school.* New York: Appleton-Century-Crofts, 1950.

Caffyn, L. Behavioral objectives: English-style. *Elementary English,* 1968, 45(8), December, 1073–74.

Canfield, A. A. A rationale for performance objectives. *Audiovisual Instruction,* 1968, 13(2), February, 127–29.

Carlisle Self-Study Project. An E.S.E.A. (Elementary and Secondary Education Act, P. L. 89-10) Title III grant to the Carlisle School District. United States Office of Education Grant No. 3729, January 1967.

Carroll, C. R. Application of the "Taxonomy of educational objectives" to alcohol education. Unpublished doctoral dissertation, Ohio State University, 1965.

Carter, H. L. Using behavioral objectives to describe stimulus similarity between assessment tasks in two content settings. Paper presented at the Annual AERA Convention, Minneapolis, March 1970.

Chambers, W. M. Testing and its relationship to educational objectives. *Journal of General Education,* 1966, 16, 246–49.

Chickering, A. W. Instructional objectives and student development in college. *Journal of Applied Behavioral Science,* 1967, 3, 287–304.

Cohen, A. M. Defining instructional objectives. In *System approaches to curriculum and instruction in open-door college.* Occasional report from U.C.L.A. Junior College Leadership Program, 1967, No. 9, January, 27–28.

Cohen, E. If you're not sure where you're going, you're liable to end up someplace else. *Media and Methods,* 1970, 6(7), March, 39–45.

Colorado State Department of Education. *Some behavioral objectives for elementary school mathematics program.* Denver, Colorado: State Department Publications, 1968.

Commission on the English Curriculum of the National Council of Teachers of English. *The English language arts in the secondary school.* New York: Appleton-Century-Crofts, 1956.

Consalvo, R. W. Evaluation and behavioral objectives. *American Biology Teacher,* 1969, 31, April, 230–32.

Cook, J. M. Behavioral objectives and rate of forgetting. Paper presented at the Annual AERA Convention, Minneapolis, March 1970.

Cook, J. M. Learning and retention by informing students of behavioral objectives and their place in the hierarchical learning sequence. Unpublished doctoral dissertation, University of Maryland, 1969.

Cox, J. A. Instructional objectives and measuring success of instruction. Symposium, Human Resources Research Office, George Washington University, Alexandria, Virginia, 1966.

Cox, R. C. Evaluative aspects of criterion-referenced measures. Paper presented at the Annual AERA Convention, Minneapolis, March 1970.

Cox, R. C. Item selection techniques and evaluation of instructional objectives. Paper presented at the Annual Meeting of the National Council on Measurement in Education, Chicago, February 1965.

Cox, R. C., & Unks, N. *A selected and annotated bibliography of studies concerning the "Taxonomy of educational objectives: Cognitive domain."* Pittsburgh: Learning Research and Development Center, University of Pittsburgh, 1967.

Cox, R. C., & Vargas, J. S. A comparison of item selection techniques for norm referenced and criterion referenced tests. Paper presented at the Annual Meeting of the National Council on Measurement in Education, Chicago, February 1966.

Craik, M. B. Writing objectives for programmed instruction—or any instruction. *Educational Technology,* 1966, 6(4), 15–20.

Crawford, M. P. Concepts of training. In Robert M. Gagné (Ed.), *Psychological principles in system development.* New York: Holt, Rinehart & Winston, 1962, 301–42.

Crawford, M. P. Research and development in training and education. Paper presented at Symposium on the Contributions of Research to Education and Training, Northwestern University, Evanston, December 1959, 22.

Crawford, M. P. Techniques in course development. Paper presented at Administrator's Training Seminar, Bureau of Personnel, U.S. Navy, Washington, May 1966.

Crawford, W. R. Assessing performance when the stakes are high. Paper presented at the Annual AERA Convention, Minneapolis, March 1970.

Crawford, W. R. A validation of the structure and generality of "A taxonomy of intellectual processes." Unpublished doctoral dissertation, Florida State University, 1966.

Cronbach, L. J. Course improvement through evaluation. *Teachers College Record,* 1963, 64, 672–83.

Danielian, J. New perspectives in training and assessment of overseas personnel. Paper read at the Counterinsurgency Research and Development Symposium, Institute for Defense Analysis, Arlington, Virginia, June 1966.

Darling, D. W. Why a taxonomy of affective learning? *Educational Leadership,* 1965, 22, 473–75.

Davis, O. L., Jr., & Tinsley, D. C. Cognitive objectives revealed by classroom questions asked by social studies student teachers. *Peabody Journal of Education,* 1967, 45, July, 21–26.

DeCecco, J. P. Educational objectives and curriculum development. *Human learning in the school.* New York: Holt, Rinehart & Winston, 1967, 566–75.

Doherty, V. W. Procedure for growth. *Educational Leadership,* 1965, 23, December, 247–49.

Dowd, D. J., & West, S. C. An inventory of measures of affective behavior. In

Improving educational assessment and an inventory of measures of affective behavior. Washington, D.C.: Association for Supervision and Curriculum Development, National Educational Association, 1969, 90–158.

Dressel, P. L. Are your objectives showing? *National Education Association Journal,* 1955, 44, 297.

Dressel, P. L. (Ed.) *Evaluation in general education.* Dubuque, Iowa: William C. Brown, 1954.

Dressel, P. L. Measurement and evaluation. In the *Yearbook of American Association of Colleges for Teacher Education.* Washington, D.C.: American Association of Colleges for Teacher Education, 1960, 45–52.

Dressel, P. L. Measurement and evaluation of instructional objectives. In *Yearbook of National Council on Measurement Used in Education.* Ames, Iowa: National Council on Measurement Used in Education, 1960, 17, 1–6.

Dressel, P. L. et al. *Evaluation in higher education.* Boston: Houghton Mifflin, 1961, Chap. 2.

Dressel, P. L., & Mayhew, L. B. *General education: Explorations in evaluation.* Washington, D.C.: American Council on Education, 1954.

Dressel, P. L., & Nelson, C. H. *Questions and problems in science,* Test Item Folio No. 1. Princeton: Educational Testing Service, 1956.

Duluth (Minn.) Public Schools. *Individualizing the instructional program,* 1966, 37. (Prepared by Thorwald Esbensen.)

Duluth (Minn.) Public Schools. *Performance objectives,* 1967, 23. (Prepared by Thorwald Esbensen.)

Dyer, H. S. Discovery and development of educational goals. *National Association of Secondary School Principals.* Washington, D.C. National Association of Secondary School Principals, National Education Association, 1967, No. 51, March, 1–14.

Ebel, R. Some limitations of criterion-referenced measurement. Paper presented at the Annual AERA Convention, Minneapolis, March 1970.

Ebel, R. L. Content standard test scores. *Educational and Psychological Measurement,* 1962, 22(1), Spring, 15–25.

Ebel, R. L. Obtaining and reporting evidence on content validity. *Educational and Psychological Measurement,* 1956, 16(3), Autumn, 269–82.

Ebel, R. L. The problem of evaluation in the social studies. *Social Education,* 1960, 24, 6–10.

Ebel, R. L. Relation of testing programs to educational goals. *National Society for the Study of Education, Yearbook, Part 2.* Chicago: University of Chicago Press, 1962, 28–44.

Edling, J. V. Educational objectives and educational media. *Review of Educational Research,* April 1968, 38(2), 177–93.

Edling, J. V. A study of the effectiveness of audiovisual teaching materials when prepared according to the principles of motivational research. (U.S. Office of Education, NDEA Title VII, Project No. 221) Monmouth, Oregon: Teaching Research Division, Oregon State System of Higher Education, June 19, 1963, 214.

Educational Evaluation. *Review of Educational Research,* 1970, 40(2), April.

Educational Policies Commission. The central purpose of American education. *National Education Association Journal,* 1961, 50(6), September, 13–16.

Educational Policies Commission. *The purposes of education in American democracy.* Washington, D.C.: American Council on Education, 1938.

Educational Policies Commission. *The unique function of education in American democracy.* Washington, D.C.: American Council on Education, 1937.

Eisner, E. W. Educational objectives: Help or hindrance? *The School Review,* Autumn, 1967, 75(3), 250–60.

Eisner, E. W. Instructional and expressive educational objectives: Their formulation and use in curriculum. In *AERA Monograph Series on Curriculum Evaluation, 3.* Chicago: Rand McNally, 1969, 1–31.

Eisner, E. W. A response to my critics. *The School Review,* Autumn 1967, 75(3), 277–82.

Elliott, C. B. Cognitive dimensions of lesson objectives set by secondary student teachers. Unpublished master's thesis, Kent State University, 1965.

Ellis, J. K. The application of the "Taxonomy of educational objectives" to the determination of objectives for health teaching. Unpublished doctoral dissertation, University of Michigan, 1963

Else, G. F. Objectives and overview. Symposium entitled Toward improvement of the high school Latin curriculum. *Classical Journal,* 1947, 43, 67–90.

Engel, R. S. An experimental study of the effects of stated behavioral objectives on achievement in a unit of instruction on negative and rational base systems of numerations. Unpublished master's thesis, University of Maryland, College Park, 1968.

Engman, B. D. Behavioral objectives: Key to planning. *The Science Teacher,* 1968, 35, October, 86–87.

Esbensen, Thorwald. Writing instructional objectives. *Phi Delta Kappan,* 1967, 48, January, 246–47.

Fenton, Edwin. *The new social studies.* New York: Holt, Rinehart & Winston, 1967, Chap. 2.

Findley, W., et al. The relation of testing programs to educational goals. In *The impact and improvement of school testing programs.* Chicago: University of Chicago Press, 1963, Part I, Chap. 2.

Findley, W. G., Frederiksen, N. O., & Saunders, D. R. *An analysis of the objectives of an executive-level educational program.* (Tech. Rep. No. 22) Maxwell Air Force Base, Alabama: Air Research and Development Command, Human Resources Institute, 1954, January, 34.

Flanagan, J. C. Contributions of research in the Army Air Forces to educational policy. *Educational Records,* 1947, 28(16), January, 78–90.

Flanagan, J. C. The critical requirements approach to educational objectives. *School and Society,* 1950, 71, 321–24.

Flanagan, J. C. Functional education for the seventies. *Phi Delta Kappan,* 1967, 49(1), September, 27–32.

Flanagan, J. C. Research techniques for developing educational objectives. *Educational Records,* 1947, 28, April, 139–48.

Florida State Department of Education. *Proposed 1968–1969 accreditation standards for Florida Schools.* Tallahassee, Florida: Florida Department of Education, 1968.

Foster, H. Categories of cognitive skills. ED 013 974. Los Angeles: University of California, November 1966.

French, W., et al. *Behavioral goals of general education in high school.* New York: Russell Sage Foundation, 1957.

Furst, E. J. *Constructing evaluation instruments.* New York: Longmans, Green, 1958.

Furst, E. J. The effect of the organization of learning experiences upon the organization of learning outcomes. *Journal of Experimental Education,* 1950, 18, 215–28, 343–52.

Gagné, R. M. The acquisition of knowledge. *Psychological Review,* 1962, 69(4), July, 355–65.

Gagné, R. M. The analysis of instructional objectives for the design of instruction. In R. L. Glaser (Ed.), *Teaching machines and programmed learning, II. Data and decisions.* Washington, D.C.: Department of Audio Visual Instruction, National Education Association, 1965, 21–65.

Gagné, R. M. *The conditions of learning.* New York: Holt, Rinehart & Winston, 1965, 172–266.

Gagné, R. M. Military training and principles of learning. *American Psychologist,* 1962, 17(2), February, 83–91.

Garvey, J. The what and why of behavioral objectives. *Instructor,* 1968, 77(8), April, 127.

Garvin, A. D. The applicability of criterion-referenced measurement by content area and level. Paper presented at the Annual AERA Convention, Minneapolis, March 1970.

Gerberich, J. R. *Measurement and evaluation in the modern school.* New York: David McKay, 1962.

Gerberich, J. R. *Specimen objective test items: A guide to achievement test construction.* New York: Longmans, Green, 1956.

Gerhand, M. Behavioral outcomes: What the child is able to do—and does—as a result of the teaching-learning experience. *Grade Teacher,* 1967, 84, 92–95.

Gerlach, V. S. Describing educational outcomes. Inglewood, California: Southwest Regional Laboratory for Educational Research and Development, 1967. (Mimeographed report)

Gerlach, V. S., & Sullivan, H. J. Constructing statements of outcomes. Inglewood, California: Southwest Regional Laboratory for Educational Research and Development, 1967. (Mimeographed report)

Glaser, R. Adapting the elementary school curriculum to individual performance. Pittsburgh, Pennsylvania: University of Pittsburgh, Learning Research and Development Center, October 1967. (Mimeographed report)

Glaser, R. The design of instruction. In *Sixty-fifth yearbook of the National Society for the Study of Education, Part II.* Chicago: University of Chicago Press, 1966.

Glaser, R. The education of individuals. Pittsburgh, Pennsylvania: University of Pittsburgh, Learning Research and Development Center, September 1966. (Mimeographed report)

Glaser, R. L. Instructional technology and the measurement of learning outcomes: Some questions. *American Psychologist,* 1963, 18, 519–21.

Glaser, R., & Cox, R. C. Criterion-referenced testing for the measurement of educational outcomes. In R. A. Weisgerber (Ed.), *Instructional process and media innovation.* Chicago: Rand McNally, 1968, 545–50.

Goals of primary education. *School and Society,* 1968, 96, Summer, 295–96.

Goodlad, J. I. Regional study centers suggested toward improved curriculum organization. *The Education Digest,* 1964, 29, February, 19–22.

Gordon, G. G., & McCormic, E. J. *A study of the activity connotations of descriptive verbs.* Indiana: Purdue University, Occupational Research Center, September, 1962, 26.

Creene, H. A. *Measurement and evaluation in the secondary school.* (2nd ed.) New York: David McKay, 1954.

Greene, H. A., & Gray, W. S. The measurement of understanding in the language arts. In *Forty-fifth yearbook of the National Society for the Study of Education, Part I.* Chicago: University of Chicago Press, 1946.

Greene, H. A., Jorgensen, A. N., & Gerberich, J. R. *Measurement and evaluation in the elementary school.* (2nd ed.) New York: David McKay, 1953.

Grieder, C. Is it possible to word educational goals? *Nations Schools,* 1961, 68, 10.

Gronlund, N. E. *Stating behavioral objectives for classroom instruction.* Toronto, Ontario: Macmillan, Collier-Macmillan Canada, Ltd., 1970.

Guide to secondary education in Oregon for school years 1957-1959. Salem, Oregon: Superintendent of Public Instruction, State Department of Educa tion, 1957, 141-42.

Gwynn, J. M. The aims-and-objectives state and activity analysis. In *Curriculum principles and social trends.* (3rd ed.) New York: Macmillan, 1960, 144-49.

Haberman, M. Behavioral objectives: Bandwagon or breakthrough. *The Journal of Teacher Education,* 1968, 19(1). Spring, 91-94.

Haehn, A. J. The design of cross-cultural training for military advisory. Paper presented at Symposium of American Psychological Association, New York, 1966.

Haehn, A. J. How to analyze performance objectives to determine training content. Research memorandum, Human Resources Research Office, George Washington University, Alexandria, Virginia, 1966.

Hammond, R. L. A design for local evaluation. *The Epic Forum.* Tucson, Arizona: Project Epic, 1967, 3-6.

Harris, C. (Ed.) *Encyclopedia of educational research.* (3rd ed.) New York: Macmillan, 1960.

Harrison, G. V. *The instructional value of presenting explicit versus vague objectives.* J. A. R. Wilson (Ed.). Santa Barbara: University of California, California Educational Research Studies, 1967.

Harvard Committee on the Objectives of Education in a Free Society. *General education in a free society.* Cambridge: Harvard University Press, 1945.

Hausdorff, H. Empirical determination of the relative importance of educational objectives. *The Journal of Experimental Education,* 1965, 34(1), Fall, 97-99.

Havighurst, R. J. Research on the developmental task concept. *School Review,* 1956, 64, 215-23.

Herrick, V. E., & Tyler, R. W. (Eds.) Toward improved curriculum theory. *Supplementary Educational Monographs.* Chicago: University of Chicago Press, 1950, No. 71.

Herron, D. J. Evaluation and the new curricula. *Journal of Research in Science Teaching,* 1966, 4, 159-70.

Higgins, M. J., & Merwin, J. C. Assessing the progress of education. *Phi Delta Kappan,* 1967, 48(8), April, 378-80.

Hill, W. F. *Learning, a survey of psychological interpretations.* San Francisco: Chandler Publishing, 1963, 2-6.

Hively, W. (Chm.) AERA Symposium entitled Domain-referenced achievement testing. Symposium presented at the Annual AERA Convention, Minneapolis, March, 1970.

Hoover, W. F. Specification of objectives. *Audiovisual Instruction,* 1967, 12, January, 597.

Horn, F. The ends for which we teach. *The Educational Forum,* 1964, 28(2), January, 133–43.

Hough, J. B. Interaction analysis in a general methods course. *Classroom Interaction Newsletter,* Temple University, 1966, 1(2), May, 7–10.

Hunkins, F. P. The influence of analysis and evaluation questions on critical thinking and achievement in sixth grade social studies. Unpublished doctoral dissertation, Kent State University, 1966.

Husek, T. R. Different kinds of evaluation and their implications for test development. *Evaluation Comment,* 1969, 2(1).

Husek, T. R., & Sirotnik, K. Item sampling in educational research. ED 013 975. Los Angeles: California University, 1957, February.

Inlow, G. M. *The emergent in curriculum.* New York: John Wiley, 1966.

Intensification of the learning process. An E.S.E.A. (Elementary and Secondary Education Act, P.L. 89–10) Title III grant to the Bucks County Schools, Raymond Bernabei, Director. United States Office of Education Grant No. 2965, August 1966.

Jackson, P. W. *The way teaching is.* Washington, D.C.: Association for Supervision and Curriculum Development, National Education Association, 1966.

Jarolimek, J. The taxonomy: Guide to differentiating instruction. *Social Education,* 1962, 26, 445–47.

Jeffries, D. J. *Lesson planning, lesson teaching.* Titusville, New Jersey: Home and School Press, 1966, 513–24.

Jenkins, J. R. Effects of instructional objectives on learning. Unpublished manuscript, University of Delaware, 1970.

Jenkins, J. R., & Deno, S. L. Effects of instructional objectives on learning. Paper presented at the Annual AERA Convention, Minneapolis, March 1970.

Johnson, P. E. The origin of item forms. Paper presented at the Annual AERA Convention, Minneapolis, March 1970.

Jones, E. M., & Fairman, J. B. Identification and analysis of human performance requirements. In John D. Folley, Jr. (Ed.), *Human factors methods for system design,* Pittsburgh: The American Institute for Research, 1960, 43–62.

Jordan, A. M. *Measurement in education.* New York: McGraw-Hill, 1953.

Joyce, B. R. Flexibility in teacher behavior. *Classroom Interaction Newsletter,* Temple University, 1967, 2(2), May, 5–12.

Judd, C. H. *Education as cultivation of the higher mental processes.* New York: Macmillan, 1936.

Kapfer, M. B. Behavioral objectives and the gifted. *Educational Technology,* 1968, 8(11), June 15, 14–15.

Kapfer, P. G. Behaviors objectives in the cognitive and affective domain. *Educational Technology,* 1968, 8(11), June 15, 11–14.

Kearney, N. C. *Elementary school objectives.* New York: Russell Sage Foundation, 1953.

Kearney, N. C. Goals of elementary education. *The National Elementary Principal,* 1954, 34, October, 12–14.

Kennedy, J. L. Psychology and system development. In R. M. Gagné (Ed.),

Psychological principles in system development. New York: Holt, Rinehart & Winston, 1962, 13–32.

Kibler, R. J., Barker, L. L., & Miles, D. T. *Behavioral objectives and instruction.* Boston: Allyn & Bacon, 1970.

Klein, S. Evaluating tests in terms of the information they provide. *Evaluation Comment,* 1970, 2(2).

Kliebhan, J. M. The effects of goal-setting and modeling on the performance of retarded adolescents in an occupational workshop. *Dissertation Abstracts,* 1967, 27(7–A), 2099–2100.

Komisar, P. B., & McClellan, J. E. Professor Arnstine and programmed instruction. *The Educational Forum,* 1965, 29, May, 467–75.

Krathwohl, D. R. Stating objectives appropriately for program, for curriculum, and for instructional materials development. *The Journal of Teacher Education,* 1965, 16, 83–92.

Krathwohl, D. R. The taxonomy of educational objectives: Its use in curriculum building. In C. M. Lindvall (Ed.), *Defining educational objectives.* Pittsburgh: University of Pittsburgh Press, 1964.

Krathwohl, D. R., Bloom, B. S., & Masia, B. B. *Taxonomy of educational objectives (The classification of educational goals), Handbook II: Affective domain.* New York: David McKay, 1964.

Lang, C. J., & Katter, R. V. A method for studying leadership. Paper presented at meeting of the American Psychological Association, Human Resources Research Office, Director of Research, George Washington University, Alexandria, Virginia, 1959.

LaPorte, W. R. The ten major objectives of health and physical education. *California Physical Education, Health and Recreation Journal,* 1936, 5, 5–6, 18.

Lazarus, A., & Knudson, R. *Selected objectives for the English arts, grades 7–12.* Boston: Houghton Mifflin, 1967.

Leavitt, H. B. Dichotomy between ends and means in American education. *Journal of Education,* 1958, 141, 14–16.

Lennon, R. T. Assumptions underlying the use of content validity. *Educational and Psychological Measurement,* 1956, 16(3), 294–304.

Lessinger, L. N. Test building and test banks through the use of the "Taxonomy of educational objectives." *California Journal of Educational Research,* 1963, 14(5), 195–201.

Lewy, A. The empirical validity of major properties of a taxonomy of affective educational objectives. *The Journal of Experimental Education,* 1968, 36(3), Spring, 70–77.

Lindquist, E. F. (Ed.) *Educational measurement.* Washington, D.C.: American Council on Education, 1951, Chaps. 5 & 6.

Lindquist, E. F. The selection of objectives. In E. F. Lindquist (Ed.), *Educational measurement.* Washington, D.C.: American Council on Education, 1951.

Lindvall, C. M. (Ed.) *Defining educational objectives.* Pittsburgh: University of Pittsburgh Press, 1964.

Lindvall, C. M. *Testing and evaluation: An introduction.* New York: Harcourt Brace, Jovanovich, 1961.

Lindvall, C. M., & Bolvin, J. L. Programmed instruction in the schools: An application of programming principles in individually prescribed instruction. In

Sixty-sixth yearbook of the National Society for the Study of Education, Part II. Chicago: University of Chicago Press, 1967.

Lipson, J. L. Individualized instruction in elementary mathematics education. In *Research in mathematics education.* Washington, D.C.: National Council of Teachers of Mathematics, 1967.

Lipson, J. L., et al. The development of an elementary school mathematics curriculum for individualized instruction. Pittsburgh, Pennsylvania: University of Pittsburgh, Learning Research and Development Center, 1966. (Mimeographed report)

Locke, E. A. Motivational effects of knowledge of results: Knowledge or goal setting? *Journal of Applied Psychology,* 1967, 51, 324-29.

Locke, E. A., & Byron, J. F. Performance goals as determinants of level of performance and boredom. *Journal of Applied Psychology,* 1967, 51, 120-30.

Lombard, J. W. Preparing better classroom tests. *The Science Teacher,* 1965, 32, October, 33-38.

A look at continuity in the school program. *1958 Yearbook Association for Supervision and Curriculum Development,* 119.

Lupold, H. F. Education with meaning: A comprehensive high school in action. *Clearinghouse,* 1967, 41, March, 440-41.

MacDonald, J. B., Andersen, D. W., & May, F. B. *Strategies of curriculum development: The works of Virgil E. Herrick.* Ohio: Charles E. Merrill, 1965.

Mager, R. F. Deriving objectives for the high school curriculum. *National Society for Programmed Instruction Journal,* 1968, 7(3), 7-14.

Mager, R. F. *Preparing instructional objectives.* Palo Alto, California: Fearon Publishers, 1962.

Maguire, T. O. Decisions and curriculum objectives: A methodology for evaluation. *Alberta Journal of Educational Research,* 1969, 16, 17-30.

Maguire, T. O. Value components of teachers' judgments of educational objectives. *Audio Visual Communication Review,* 1968, 16(1), Spring, 63-74.

Marks, J. L., Puroy, C. R., & Kinney, L. B. *Teaching arithmetic for understanding.* New York: McGraw-Hill, 1958, 343-44.

Marksberry, M. L., et al. Relation between cognitive objectives from selected texts and from recommendations of national committees. *Journal of Educational Research,* 1969, 62, 422-29.

Marsh, C. S. *American universities and colleges.* Washington, D.C.: American Council on Education, 1936, 7-8, 17, 31, 47-49.

May, K. O. Programming and mathematics teaching. *The Education Digest,* 1966, 32, October, 38-41.

Mayer, F. Aims of education. *Education,* 1956, 76, 630-38.

Mayor, J. R. Science and mathematics in the elementary school. *The Arithmetic Teacher,* 1967, 14(8), December, 629-35.

McAshan, H. H. *Writing behavioral objectives: A new approach.* New York: Harper & Row, 1970.

McAulay, J. D. Criteria for elementary social studies. *Educational Leadership,* 1968, 25(7), April, 651-55.

McFann, H. F. Individualization of instruction. Paper presented at Human Factors Research and Development Conference, Fort Benning, Georgia, October 1966.

McGrath, D. (Ed.) *A design for general education.* Washington, D.C.: American Council on Education, 1944.

McGrath, J. E., Nordlie, P. G., & Vaughan, W. S., Jr. A systematic framework for comparison of system research methods. Arlington, Virginia: Human Sciences Research, 1960, Report No. 1, March.

McMurrin, S. M. What tasks for the schools? *Saturday Review,* 1967, 50(2), January 14, 40–43.

McNeil, J. D. Antidote to a school scandal. *Educational Forum,* 1966, 31, November, 69–77.

McNeil, J. D. Concomitants of using behavioral objectives in the assessment of teacher effectiveness. *Journal of Experimental Education,* 1967, 36(1), 69–71.

McSwain, E. T., & Cooke, R. J. *Understanding and teaching arithmetic in the elementary school.* New York: Holt, Rinehart & Winston, 1958, 333–34.

Melching, W. H. In defense of instructional objectives. Symposium, Human Resources Research Office, George Washington University, Alexandria, Virginia, 1966.

Melching, W. H., et al. *Deriving, specifying and using instructional objectives.* (Tech. Rep. No. 10-66) Alexandria, Virginia: Human Resources Research Office, George Washington University, December 1966.

Melching, W. H., et al. *A handbook for programmers of automated instruction.* Fort Bliss, Texas: U.S. Army Air Defense Human Research Unit, September 1963.

Melching, W. H., et al. *The text of an orientation workshop in automated instruction.* Fort Bliss, Texas: U.S. Army Air Defense Human Research Unit, July 1962.

Melching, W.H., & Ammerman, H. L. *The derivation, analysis and classification of instructional objectives.* (Tech. Rep. No. 66-4) Alexandria, Virginia: Human Resources Research Office, George Washington University, 1966.

Messick, S. The criterion problem in the evaluation of instruction: Assessing possible, not just intended, outcomes. (Also, comments by Paul Blomers.) Los Angeles: University of California, Center for the Study of Evaluation of Instructional Programs, 1969, May. ED 030 987, ED 030 980.

Metfessel, N. S., & Michael, W. B. A paradigm involving multiple criterion measures for the evaluation of the effectiveness of school programs. *Educational and Psychological Measurement,* 1967, 27, 931–43 (373–83).

Metfessel, N. S., Michael, W. B., & Kirsner, D. A. Instrumentation of Bloom's and Krathwohl's taxonomies for the writing of educational objectives. *Psychology in the Schools,* 1969, 6(3), 227–31.

Miller, J. N. New cure for boredom in the classroom. *The Reader's Digest,* 1966, May, 171–72. Condensed from the *PTA Magazine.*

Miller, R. B. Analysis and specification of behavior for training. In Robert Glaser (Ed.), *Training research and education.* Pittsburgh: University of Pittsburgh Press, 1962, 31–62.

Miller, R. B. Some working concepts of systems analysis. Pittsburgh: American Institute for Research, February 1954.

Miller, R. B. Task description and analysis. In Robert M. Gagné (Ed.), *Psychological principles in system development.* New York: Holt, Rinehart & Winston, 1962, 187–299.

Millman, J. Reporting student progress: A case for a criterion- referenced marking system. Paper presented at the Annual AERA Convention, Minneapolis, March 1970.

Mitchell, J. M. A study of a systematic method of teaching: Contributions to education. George Peabody College for Teachers, 1929, No. 61.

Monroe, W. S. *Directing learning in the high school.* Garden City, New York: Doubleday, Doran & Co., 1927, 51–114, 539–70.

Monroe, W. S. *Measuring the results of teaching.* New York: Houghton Mifflin, 1918, 267–80.

Monroe, W. S., & Engelhart, M. D. *The scientific study of educational problems.* New York: Macmillan, 1936, 411–13, 419–35.

Monroe, W. S., Hindman, D. A., & Lundin, R. S. Two illustrations of curriculum construction. *University of Illinois Bulletin, 25(26), Bureau of Educational Research Bulletin, No. 39.* Urbana, Illinois: University of Illinois, 1928.

Monroe, W. S., Odell, C. W., Herriott, M. E., Engelhart, M. D., & Hull, M. R. Ten years of educational research, 1918–1927. *Bureau of Educational Research Bulletin,* No. 42. Urbana, Illinois: University of Illinois, College of Education, 1928, 116–38.

Monroe, W. S., & Weber, O. F. *The high school.* Garden City, New York: Doubleday, Doran & Co., 1928, 122–226, 437–67.

Montague, E. J., & Butts, D. P. Behavioral objectives. *Science Teacher,* 1968, 35(3), March, 33–35.

Morse, H. T., & McCune, G. H. *Selected items for the testing of study skills.* Washington, D.C.: National Council for the Social Studies, National Educational Association, 1949, Bulletin No. 15.

Muthersbaugh, G. C. Objectives of a proposed course of study in physics for senior high schools. *School Science and Mathematics,* 1929, 29, December, 743–54.

National Education Association Educational Policies Commission. *The central purpose of American education.* Washington, D.C.: National Education Association, 1961, 4.

National Education Association Research Division. A new look at the seven cardinal principles of education. *Journal of the National Education Association,* 1967, 56, January, 53–54.

National Society for the Study of Education. *The measurement of understanding. Forty-fifth yearbook, Part I.* Chicago: University of Chicago Press, 1946.

Nault, W. H. *Typical course of study, kindergarten through grade 12.* Chicago: Field Enterprises Educational Corporation, 1966.

Nedelsky, L. Absolute grading standards for objective tests. *Educational and Psychological Measurement,* 1954, 14, 3–19.

Nerbovig, M. H. Teachers' perceptions of the function of objectives. *Dissertation Abstracts,* 1956, 16(12), 2406–07.

Nitko, A. J. Criterion-referenced testing in the context of instruction. Paper presented at the Educational Records Bureau—National Council on Measurement in Education Symposium, entitled Criterion-referenced measures: Pros and cons. New York, 1970.

Nitko, A. J. Some considerations when using a domain-referenced system of achievement tests in instructional situations. Paper presented at the Annual AERA Convention, Minneapolis, March 1970.

Noll, V. H. The objectives of science instruction. In *Science education in American schools. Forty-sixth yearbook of the National Society for the Study of Education, Part I.* Chicago: University of Chicago Press, 1947, 28–29.

Nuthall, G. *University of Illinois project on the strategies of teaching.* United States Department of Health, Education and Welfare, Office of Education, Cooperative Research Project No. 1640.

Oakleaf Elementary School. *Behavioral objectives for reading.* Pittsburgh, Pennsylvania: Baldwin-Whitehall School District publication.

Oakleaf Elementary School. *Mathematics continuum.* Pittsburgh, Pennsylvania: Baldwin-Whitchall School District publication.

Odiorne, G. S. *Management by objectives, a system of managerial leadership.* New York: Pitman Co., 1965.

Ohnmacht, F. W. Factor analysis of ranked educational objectives: An approach to value orientation. *Educational and Psychological Measurement,* 1965, 25(2), 437–47.

Ojemann, R. H. Should educational objectives be stated in behavioral terms? *The Elementary School Journal,* 1968, 68, 223–31; 1969, 69, 229–35.

Oswald, J. M. Problems posed by instructional objectives in curriculum. Occasional paper. Syracuse. Syracuse University Social Science Education Curriculum Center.

Oswald, J. M. Some effects of instructor specified instructional objectives on achievement of knowledge and comprehension. Unpublished doctoral dissertation, Stanford University, 1970.

Oswald, J. M., & Fletcher, J. D. On objectives. Paper presented at the Annual AERA Convention, Minneapolis, March 1970.

Palmer, R. R. Evaluating school objectives. *Education Research Bulletin,* 1958, 37, 60–66.

Paulson, C. F. Slide presentation on writing behavioral objectives. Monmouth, Oregon: Oregon State System of Higher Education, Teaching Research Division.

Paulson, C. F. Specifying behavioral objectives. *National Research Training Institute Manual for Participants in Research Development (CORD) Projects.* Monmouth, Oregon: Oregon State System of Higher Education, Teaching Research Division, 1967, Part II, August, 1–13.

Paulson, R. F. Objectives of education. In *American Education—Challenges and Images.* Tucson, Arizona: The University of Arizona Press, 1967.

Peters, C. C. *Objectives and procedures in civic education.* New York: Longmans, Green, 1930, 302.

Pfeiffer, I. L. Teaching in ability-grouped English classes: A study of verbal interaction and cognitive goals. *Journal of Experimental Education,* 1967, 36(1), 33–38.

Pfeiffer, I., & Davis, O. L., Jr. Teacher-made examination: What kinds of thinking do they demand? *Bulletin of the National Association of Secondary School Principals,* 1965, 49, September, 1–10.

Plowman, P. *Behavioral objectives extension service.* Chicago: Science Research Associates, 1968-69.

Popham, W. J. Educational needs assessment in the cognitive, affective, and psycho-motor domain. Los Angeles: University of California at Los Angeles, Center for the Study of Evaluation.

Popham, W. J. *Educational objectives.* Los Angeles: A filmstrip-tape program produced by Vimcet Associates, 1967.

Popham, W. J. Focus on outcomes, a guiding theme of ES '70 schools. *Phi Delta Kappan,* 1969, 51(4), 208–10.

Popham, W. J. Indices of adequacy for criterion-referenced test items. Paper presented at the Annual AERA Convention, Minneapolis, March 1970.

Popham, W. J. Instructional objectives, 1960–1970. Address presented at the Eighth Annual Convention of the National Society for Programmed Instruction, Anaheim, California, May 1970.

Popham, W. J. Objectives and instruction. In *AERA Monograph Series on Curriculum Evaluation, 3*. Chicago: Rand McNally, 1969, 32–62.

Popham, W. J. The performance test: A new approach to the assessment of teaching proficiency. *The Journal of Teacher Education*, 1968, 19, 216–22.

Popham, W. J. Probing the validity of arguments against behavioral goals. Paper presented at the Annual AERA Convention, Chicago, February 1968.

Popham, W. J. Selecting appropriate educational objectives. Los Angeles: A filmstrip-tape program produced by Vimcet Associates, 1967.

Popham, W. J., & Baker, E. L. Curriculum principles for prospective teachers. *Teacher Education Quarterly*, 1965, 22, 38–41.

Popham, W. J., & Baker, E. L. The instructional objectives preference test. *Journal of Educational Measurement*, 1965, 2, 186.

Popham, W. J., & Baker, E. L. Measuring teachers' attitudes toward behavioral objectives. *The Journal of Educational Research*, 1967, 60, 453–55.

Popham, W. J., & Baker, E. L. *Systematic instruction.* New York: Prentice-Hall, 1970.

Popham, W. J., Eisner, E. W., Sullivan, H. J., & Tyler, L. L. In *AERA Monograph Series on Curriculum Evaluation, 3*. Chicago: Rand McNally, 1969.

Popham, W. J., & Husek, T. R. Implications of criterion-referenced measurement. *Journal of Educational Measurement*, 1969, 6, 1–10.

Popham, W. J., & Skager, R. Instructional objectives measurement system. *Progress in evaluation study.* Third annual report to the U.S. Office of Education. Los Angeles: Center for the Study of Evaluation, University of California, 1968.

Powers, T. R. The development of a basis for a common core curriculum. Paper read at meeting of American Psychological Association, Director of Research, Human Resources Research Office, Fort Benning, Georgia, 1965.

President's Commission on Higher Education. *Establishing the goals.* Vol. 1. Washington, D.C.: Government Printing Office, 1947.

Pullen, T. G., Jr. Defining goals of public education. *Baltimore Bulletin of Education*, 1959, 36, 30–32.

Quillen, I. J. Evaluating objectives of education in American life. *Educational Record*, 1958, 39, 222–29.

Rabehl, G. J. The MINNEMAST experiment with domain referenced achievement testing. Paper presented at Annual AERA Convention, Minneapolis, March 1970.

Rahmlow, H. F. Specifying useful instructional objectives. *National Society for Programmed Instruction Journal*, 1968, 7(7), 10–15.

Raths, J. D. Specificity as a threat to curriculum reform. Paper presented at the Annual AERA Convention, Chicago, February 1968.

Raths, L. Basis for comprehensive evaluation. *Educational Research Bulletin*, 1936, 17, 57–84.

Remmers, H. H., & Gage, N. L. *Educational measurement and evaluation.* (Rev. ed.) New York: Harper and Row, 1955, Chap. 2.

Remmers, H. H., Gage, N. L., & Rummel, J. F. *A practical introduction to measurement and evaluation.* (2nd ed.) New York: Harper and Row, 1965, 181–207.

Romberg, T. A. The development of mathematics achievement tests for the national longitudinal study of mathematical abilities. Leland Stanford Junior University, 1966. (Mimeographed report)

Romberg, T., & Kilpatrick, J. Preliminary study on evaluation in mathematics education. Leland Stanford Junior University, 1966. (Mimeographed report)

Sand, O. Schools for the 70's. *The National Elementary Principal,* 1967, 47(1), September, 21–29.

Scannell, D. P., & Stillwagen, W. R. Teaching and testing for degrees of understanding. *California Journal of Instructional Improvement,* 1960.

Schaefer, M. G. Revision of secondary mathematics in a selected number of schools. *The Mathematics Teacher,* 1968, 61(2), February, 157–61.

Scriven, M. *Student values as educational objectives.* Boulder: Social Sciences Educational Consortium, University of Colorado, 1966, Publication No. 124.

Searles, J. E. *System for instruction.* New York: Intext, 1967.

Shriver, E. L. Determining training requirements for electronic system maintenance: Development and test of a new method of skill and knowledge analysis. (Tech. Rep. 63) Washington, D.C.: Human Resources Research Office, Alexandria, Virginia, June 1960. (Reissued in August 1963)

Simpson, E. J. *The classification of educational objectives: Psychomotor domain.* U.S. Department of Health, Education, and Welfare, Office of Education, Vocational and Technical Education Grant Contract No. OE 5-85-104. Urbana: University of Illinois, 1966.

Skager, R. W., & Broadbent, L. A. Cognitive structures and educational evaluation. ERIC: ED 016 282. Los Angeles: University of California, 1967, April.

Slack, C. W. The politics of educational objectives. *Educational Technology,* 1967, 7(14), July 30, 1–6.

Smith, E. R., & Tyler, R. W. *Appraising and recording student progress.* New York: Harper & Row, 1942.

Smith, S. A. The effects of two variables on the achievement of slow learners on a unit in mathematics. Unpublished master's thesis, The University of Maryland, College Park, 1967.

Stake, R. E. The countenance of educational evaluation. *Teachers College Record,* 1967, 68, 523–40.

Stake, R. E., & Gooler, D. Measuring educational priorities. Paper presented at the Annual AERA Convention, Minneapolis, March 1970.

Stasiewski, A. Setting a course for yourself and your students. *Grade Teacher,* 1967, 84, April, 96–97.

Stoker, H. W., & Kropp, R. P. Measurement of cognitive processes. *Journal of Educational Measurement,* 1964, 1(1), 39–42.

Suchman, R. J. Old goals and new perspectives. *Instructor,* 1967, 76(5), January, 23.

Sulzer, J. L., & Levy, C. M. Goal and error training methods in the learning of positioning response. *Psychonomic Science,* 1966, 6, 179–80.

Swintti, R. L. Certain effects of training goals on subsequent task performance. *Occupational Psychology,* 1966, 40, 153–65.

Taber, J. I., Glaser, R., & Schaifer, H. *Learning and programmed instruction.* Reading, Mass.: Addison-Wesley, 1965, Chap. 4.

Taylor, P. A., & Maguire, T. O. Perceptions of some objectives for a science curriculum. *Science Education,* 1967, 51, 488–93.

Thayer, V. T., Zachry, C. B., & Kotinsky, R. *Reorganizing secondary education.* New York: Appleton-Century-Crofts, 1939.

Thomas, R. M. *Judging student progress.* New York: Longmans, Green, 1954.

Tonne, H. A., Popham, E. L., & Freeman, M. H. *Methods of teaching business subjects.* New York: McGraw-Hill, 1949.

Travers, R. M. V. *Educational measurement.* New York: Macmillan, 1955, 94–115.

Trow, W. C. Behavioral objectives in education. *Educational Technology,* 1967, 7(24), December 30, 6–10.

Trow, W. C. Grades and objectives in higher education. *Educational Record,* 1968, 49(1), Winter, 85–91.

Trow, W. C. On marks, norms, and proficiency scores. *Phi Delta Kappan,* 1966, 48(4), December, 171–73.

Tuckman, B. W. A taxonomy for classifying educational-relevant behaviors. Paper presented at the Annual AERA Convention, Minneapolis, March, 1970.

Twelker, P. A. Objective analysis and instructional specification. *National Research Training Institute Manual for Participants in Research Development (CORD) Projects.* Monmouth, Oregon: Oregon State System of Higher Education, Teaching Research Division, 1967, Part III, August, 1–19.

Tyler, L. L. Symposium on the instructional objectives controversy. Paper presented at the meeting of the National Council on Measurement in Education, 1968.

Tyler, L. L., & Okumu, L. J. A beginning step: A system for analyzing courses in teacher education. *Journal of Teacher Education,* 1965, 16(4), 438–44.

Tyler, R. W. *Basic principles of curriculum and instruction.* Chicago: University of Chicago Press, 1950.

Tyler, R. W. *Constructing achievement tests.* Columbus: Ohio State University Press, 1934.

Tyler, R. W. Evaluating the elementary school. *National Elementary Principal,* 1964, 43(6), May, 9–13.

Tyler, R. W. The functions of measurement in improving instruction. In Lindquist, E. F. (Ed.), *Educational measurement.* Washington: American Council of Education, 1951, 47–67.

Tyler, R. W. A generalized technique for construction of achievement tests. *Educational Research Bulletin,* 1931, 10, 199–208.

Tyler, R. W. Some persistent questions on the defining of objectives. In Lindvall, C. M. (Ed.), *Defining educational objectives.* Pittsburgh: University of Pittsburgh Press, 1964, 77–83.

Tyler, R. W., Gagné, R., & Scriven, M. In *AERA Monograph on Perspectives of Curriculum Evaluation. 1.* Chicago: Rand McNally, 1967.

U.S. Department of Interior, Bureau of Education. *Cardinal principles of education,* 1918, Bulletin 38.

Vaughn, K. W. Planning the objective list. In Lindquist, E. F. (Ed.), *Educational measurement.* Washington, D.C.: American Council on Education, 1951, 159–84.

Walbesser, H. H. (Chm.) AERA Symposium entitled Behavioral objectives and learning hierarchies. Symposium presented at the Annual AERA Convention, Minneapolis, March 1970.

Walbesser, H. H. *Constructing behavioral objectives.* College Park: The Bureau of Educational Research and Field Services, University of Maryland, 1968.

Walbesser, H. H. Curriculum evaluation by means of behavioral objectives. *Journal of Research in Science Teaching,* 1963, 1, 296–301.

Walker, D. F. A study of types of goal statements and their uses in a curriculum development project. Paper presented at the Annual AERA Convention, Minneapolis, March 1970.

Washburne, C., & Marland, S. D., Jr. *Winnetka: The history and significance of an educational experiment.* Englewood Cliffs: Prentice-Hall, 1963.

Whitford, W. G. *An introduction of art education.* New York: Century Co., 1929, 120–22.

Whitmore, P. G. The content validity of instructional objectives. Symposium, Human Resources Research Office, George Washington University, Alexandria, Virginia, 1966.

Whitmore, P. G. Deriving and specifying instructional objectives. Paper read at Symposium on Automated Teaching: Research problem. Meeting of American Psychological Association, September 1961.

Whitmore, P. G. A rational analysis of the process of instruction. *IRE Transaction on Education,* 1961, December, 135–43.

Wildman, P. R. The fallacy of facts. *Peabody Journal of Education,* 1966, 44, November, 177–80.

Wilson, R. C. Improving criteria for complex mental processes. In *Proceedings of the 1957 Invitational Conference on Testing Problems.* Princeton, N.J.: Educational Testing Service, 1957.

Wisconsin Department of Public Instruction, *K–6: Guidelines to mathematics.* Madison Wisconsin: State Department publication, 1966.

Wise, L. E. Stop teaching Biology. *Education Digest,* 1966, 32, October, 52–54.

Wolf, R. Review of The construction and validation of tests of the cognitive processes as described in the taxonomy of educational objectives. *Educational and Psychological Measurement,* 1967, 27, 542–48.

Woodring, P. Subject matter and the goals of education. *Educational Forum,* 1960, 24, 417–19.

Wrightstone, J. W., Justman, J., & Robbins, I. *Evaluation in modern education.* New York: American Book Co., 1956, Chap. 2.